FOLK-TALES OF ASSAM

FOLK-TALES OF ASSAM

BY

JNANADABHIRAM BARUA

GYAN

Published by

Gyan Publishing House
5, Ansari Road
Daryaganj, New Delhi-110002
Phone: 011-47034999, 9811692060
E-mail: books@gyanbooks.com

Distribution Network
gyanbooks.com
India, USA, Canada, UK, Australia

ISBN: 978-93-6280-290-3 (PB)
First Published, 1963

2nd Impression 2024

Printed at: Gyan Press, Delhi.

FOLK TALES OF ASSAM
Author: JNANADABHIRAM BARUA

FOLK-TALES OF ASSAM

BY

JNANADABHIRAM BARUA

J. BOROOAH

BARRISTER-AT-LAW

PREFACE

I shall be failing in my duty if I do not thank my friend Mr. Lakshminath Bezbaroa B.A. for his so kindly allowing me to translate some of the tales from his Assamese compilation *Burhi Air Sadhu* (which literally translated would mean Tales of a Grandmother). I hereby tender my best thanks to Mr. Bezbaroa.

Mr. Bezbaroa is well-known in Assam and to all readers of Assamese literature. He has enriched the literature of Assam by his inimitable writings. He is also the Editor of a very widely circulated Assamese monthly publication (*Banhi*). Long may he live to enrich our language.

I bring out this publication with a great deal of hesitation, for it is well-known that the translator's work is beset with a great many difficulties. To begin with, I am translating from my own language into a language which is not my own. Innumerable defects of expressions and idioms therefore may have crept in, but notwithstanding such defects I have not the slightest doubt that even a casual reader will be able to follow the language without any difficulty.

I have tried, as far as possible, to translate the tales literally. This may have marred the style, but I wanted to lay before the readers, if any, of these translations, the exact method how a tale is told by an Assamese I do not know if I have succeeded in my attempt.

My thanks are also due to those friends who have, from time to time, helped me with their advice in the course of my work.

With all their imperfections due to their new garb I present these tales to the kind indulgence of my readers

I now offer this book to the general public. I sincerely hope my readers will like these tales.

Earle Law College,
Gauhati
in the autumnal
season of 1915

J. Borooah

PREFACE TO THE SECOND EDITION

The first edition was published by the Timber & Stores Agency (22, Rosemary Lane, Howrah), Mr. Lakshminath Bezbaroa's firm in 1915. I had intended these translations for the children and "grown ups" of the English-speaking world. My idea was to place our Assamese folk-tales before the world so that they might gain some knowledge about Assam.

Mr Bichitra Narayan Dutta Borooah, B. L., of Lawyer's Book Stall, Gauhati has undertaken to publish this edition very kindly. As this book will receive excellent treatment from him I need no further comments

I have now very great pleasure in offering this book **to the children, young and old, of the English speaking world.**

God bless them

ব্ৰহ্মকৃপাহিকেৱলম্

(ब्रह्मकृपाहिकेवलम्)

Abhiram,
Gauhati, Assam
25th October, 1954

J. Borooah

PUBLISHER'S NOTE

SECOND EDITION

FOLK-TALES OF ASSAM by Sri Jnanadabhiram Borooah, Bar-at-Law, is now before tht public, revised and illustrated.

FOLK-TALES, more than anything else, reflect the mind of a people Assam is rich in these but at one period of her history they were well-nigh being forgotten

A true Assamese that Sri Borooah was after his return from England, he undertook to reconstruct the scattered threads of our folk-tales, and in 1915 he brought out the first edition of FOLK-TALES OF ASSAM

Vicissitudes of fortune caused the eclipse of this slim though valuable book, and it is only last year that Sri Borooah placed the charge of its reprinting and republication with us.

As a result of that trust, we had the book revised by Dr. Praphulladatta Goswami, who has not however made any major alterations. Some pictures have also been added in this edition

Unfortunately, during progress of its publication, Sri Borooah passed away on 27th January last, and this valuable national property remains to be his posthumus child

BICHITRA NARAYAN DATTA BOROOAH

CONTENTS

1. The Tale Of The Cat's Daughter ... 1
2. The Monkey And The Fox ... 8
3. The Ow Princess 15
4. The Jungle Crow And The Wren ... 20
5. A Flower Maiden And A Flower Plant 26
6. The Tale Of A Cunning Fox ... 29
7 The Tale Of The Tiger And The Crab 36
8 Tejimala 51
9 The Old Man, The Old Woman And The Fox ... 62
10. The Long-Legged One ... 67
11 The Globefish . .. 73
12. The Youngest Child 79
13. The All-Knowing One ... 84
14. The Tale Of A Singara Fish ... 94
15. The Tale Of A Strong Man ... 98
16. The Tale Of The Kite's Daughter 103
17 Toola And Teja 117

FOLK-TALES OF ASSAM

The Tale of the Cat's Daughter

(Mekuri Jiyekar Sadhu)

Once upon a time a farmer had a pet cat who was about to kitten. The farmer's wife was with child at the same time. The cat wanted very much to eat fish and said to the farmer's wife. "I am longing to cat fish badly" She replied, "Child, you must get me the fish first, then I shall let you have it, otherwise where am I to get any fish ?" Hearing this the cat began from that very day to bring her fish somehow or other, stealing here and robbing there.

Now the mistress of the house used to cook and eat fish every day leaving the cat only the bones. So although the cat had to find the fish, she got none of it herself. This made her very angry and she cursed the farmer's wife saying, "What I am carrying may she carry and what she is carrying may I carry." After this the mistress actually gave birth to two kittens and the cat to two little girls. The cat brought the children up with love and care She used to go out in search of fish and milk daily leaving the children behind at home. When they grew up, one day they said to her, "Mother, if by chance you happen to be killed on your way to and from our village, how shall we know of it and what shall we do then ?" The mother, placing a tulasi plant* and a saucer of milk in the room, replied, "If any one kills me the tulasi plant will wither and the milk will turn black. Go in search of me then" A few days after this the tulasi did wither and the milk did turn black, upon which the two little girls went out in search of their mother, thinking, some evil had befallen her After they had gone a long way, the younger sister felt thirsty. Presently, they came to a river, and leaving her on the bank the elder sister went to fetch some water First she had a drink herself, then as she was going to take some water for her sister the river dried up, and the river-god called

* Tulasi plant—the holy basil, called *tulsi* in Hindi

out, "If you will give me the ring on your finger I will give you some water."

Could the ring be more valuable to her than her sister ? So she dropped it into the river and took some water in exchange.

After the younger sister had her drink of water she sent the elder back to the river to get the ring , but as soon as she got into the water she was carried away by the river-god There-upon the younger sister began to beat her breast and cry bitterly

A little later, a merchant who was passing that way with his merchandise saw a beautiful girl sitting alone on the bank, took her into his boat and sailed away When he reached home he made her his wife He had already two wives but he loved his little wife more than the others So they became jealous, and began to plan some means of making the merchant hate her When her first child was born she was blindfolded by them, and they threw the little baby into the river saying that she had given birth to a flail for pounding rice. Next time they did the same thing with the child and said that she had given birth to a pumpkin.

Now the girl who was carried off by the river-god, recognising these children to be her sister's, brought them up and took care of them. But the merchant, believing that his youngest wife had actually given birth to these strange things, thought that she was an unlucky woman and

drove her out of the house. She was given a hut to live in, right away near the dunghill, and there she lived on in misery and sorrow

One day when the merchant was going in a boat the river-god stopped it in midstream. When he was at a loss as to what to do, some one from the bottom of the river called out, "If you undertake to call all the people together and let me know when they will meet, and throw into the water as a pledge of good faith your areca-nut-carrier and stick, then I shall let your boat go—otherwise not." The merchant having done as he was told the boat was allowed to go on.

Now their aunt told the children the whole story from the time of their mother being born of the cat to the time when they were thrown into the river, and they were told to repeat it at the great meeting called by their father On the day of the gathering they made their way to the merchant's house, and took the areca-nut-carrier and the stick with them As soon as ever they got there they ran to the hut where their mother was living and said, "Mother, give us some water," as they were thirsty

The poor woman, never having been called "Mother" by anyone before, thought they were making fun of her and said, "Why tease me , go to the great big meeting and there eat and drink whatever you want "

Then they told her the whole story and who they were and after staying a while with her went to the meeting.

The people there began saying that two strangers were present who were seen to have taken food and drink in the evil woman's hut and everybody insisted on knowing who they were

Upon this both the brothers stood up at once and said, "The lady at whose hut we were seen is our mother" When they all asked the merchant if he knew anything about it he could give no explanation Then the brothers were asked for an explanation. The elder one told his tale from the very beginning, explaining every detail and showed the areca-nut-carrier and the stick to prove the truth of his story.

The merchant was thunderstruck and he admitted that the things were his. Then everybody came to know of the wickedness of the two elder wives who on being asked for an explanation remained silent After the meeting broke up, the merchant chopped off the ears and noses of his two wives and drove them out of the house—and he lived happily with the two boys and their mother ever after

The Monkey And The Fox

(Bandar Aru Shial)

Once upon a time there lived a monkey and a fox who were great friends. They put their heads together and laid plans to roam about and get plenty to eat One day as they were arranging the day's plans sitting by a road in the woods they saw some men coming towards them with loads of bananas, milk, treacle, sugar-cane and various dainties for a marriage feast On seeing them the fox said to the monkey, "Friend, you see those things carried by the men We must have them, at any cost ; let us find out some means of doing so. You had better hide yourself under a tree near the road at a little distance, and I shall hide near here. When they come near us I shall shout *howa,* and you from your place must shout *khowa,* and you may be sure that on hearing us shout so suddenly they will take fright and run away"

When the men approached them the woods rang with their *howa-howas* and *khowa-khowas.* Thinking that either tigers or bears were about to fall upon them the men left their loads then and there and took to their heels. Seeing them run away like that both the fox and the monkey were wild with joy, and made off with their booty to the jungle. The monkey then said to the fox, "Friend, if we sit here and begin to eat and the men come back to look for their things, there will be an end of us both, and we shall lose everything into the bargain Let us then do this ; I had better climb to the top of this tree with these things and you had better remain below, for you can't climb trees ; you know, after taking my share I shall throw you yours. So like a good chap lend me a hand in lifting these things from the ground and I shall carry them up" The fox, agreeing to this proposal, lifted the things one by one for the monky and the latter climbed up the tree with them

When he had safely carried up everything, the monkey, quite happy and serene, went on eating to his heart's content The fox from the bottom of the tree called out, "Friend, where is my share ?" The monkey, after eating a banana threw the skin down to the fox saying, "Here friend, catch, there goes a banana." After drinking off the milk he threw the can down saying, "Friend, here goes your share of the milk, mind you catch it." After sucking the juice of the sugar-cane he threw the fibre down saying, "There goes a

sugar-cane, friend, catch it" When the fox saw how he was being done in the eye by the monkey, in his impotent rage he began to scratch the ground with his paws and bite the bark of the tree and then left the place.

One day the monkey saw the fox sitting near a nest of hornets He came up to him and asked, "Friend, what are you doing ?" The fox replied, "Friend, it is just my luck I can't help it, the king has appointed me the keeper of his drums, that is why I am sitting here in charge of this one." The monkey said, "Do let me have a beat at it like a good chap." "Friend, it is entirely out of the question," the fox replied ; "I can't let you do it—if the king were to hear of it I shall be cut in two Can't you hear friend, the drum is so good that it is giving out a soft musical sound even when it is not beaten ?" Said the monkey, "Do friend, do let me just touch it, only a gentle touch, the king won't know I am longing to play it." The fox said, "Friend, it is impossible to refuse you really—well, you may just play the drum gently ; gently, mind you." and then disappeared all on a sudden As soon as the monkey struck at the hornet's nest, he was surrounded on all sides by hundreds of angry hornets who stung his hands, feet, mouth, in short, all over his body. The monkey, quite confounded and rolling and writhing about in pain cried out,

"Friend, come and help me, I am dying." The fox from a safe distance replied, "Didn't you throw me the peel after finishing the banana ?

I am just paying a compliment in return" The monkey cried, "Friend, save me, I am dying." The fox replied, "I am just giving you tit for tat in return for the can without the milk" The monkey cried, "Friend, do, do come, I am dying." The fox replied, "I am just taking my revenge for your throwing me the fibre after sucking the juice of the sugar-cane, that is all" Saying this, he left the place leaving the monkey to his fate

Long after this the monkey saw the fox keeping watch over a plot of land with poisonous arum plants. The monkey had quite forgotten about the hornets. He came up to the fox and asked, "Friend, what are you doing ? What are these plants ?" The fox turned towards the monkey and replied smiling, "This is the king's sugar-cane plantation and every cane is ripe for eating. I have been appointed to keep watch over it by Royal command. The king's commands have to be obeyed—what is to be done ?" The mention of sugarcane made the monkey's mouth water He asked, "Friend, could you just let me taste a tiny winny one ?" The fox replied, "What are yau talking about, friend ? They belong to the king, and if he were to hear of my letting you taste these sugar-canes he will not only kill me but kill my little ones also." The greedy monkey again said, "Friend, I am longing for a taste, do let me have one, just one on the sly,—the king won't know." The fox said, "If you are so eager to, do have one, mind you, one only and no more I will bear any punishment that is given me for your sake" As soon as he got permission, the greedy monkey broke a big arum stem and started munching away. The arum did its work and his mouth began to itch and smart all over. He was sorely distressed and shrieked out, "Friend, save me, I am dying." The fox replied, "A return compliment for the peel you threw me after eating up the banana" The monkey called out, "Friend, I am dying.' The fox replied, "I am just revenging myself for your throwing me the fibre after sucking the sugarcane." The monkey again cried, "Friend, come and save me" The fox said, "I am giving you tit for tat for the jar thrown down after you finished the treacle" and left the spot.

A long time after this the monkey in his wanderings came across the fox seated by the side of an old well. The mouth of the well was covered with cobwebs The monkey having forgotten all that had happened before asked the fox what he was doing The fox replied, "Ah, friend, the worry of it, I always somehow or other have to do with something or other in the king's household. This is our princess's sedan-chair which she got for her dowry and I am in charge of it." The monkey said, "It is great fun riding in the king's sedan-chair. is not it, friend? Let me see what it is like to ride in it, do." The fox replied, "I can't allow that, friend. If the king were to find the slightest sign of its having been used, I shall get the sack" The monkey said, "What possible trace could he find? I shall just get in and get down very gently" The fox replied, "If you are really so anxious to have a ride, do so at once before any one sees you." The monkey thinking he was about to enjoy a ride in the Royal sedan-chair, put on a grand air ; but soon as he sat on it, the cobwed gave way and falling into the well he was drowned.

The Ow Princess

(Ow Kooanri)

A certain king had two queens. Both of them were with child and were delivered of on the same day The elder queen had a boy and the younger an acid fruit called *ow*. The latter was much grieved to find that she was delivered of a fruit only and she threw it into the place where refuse and offals were thrown But when the queen was busy at work or would go to bed, the *ow* would roll into where she used to be. It would keep on rolling back near her even when she would throw it out. One midday when none was about, the *ow* rolled on to the steps leading to the bathing ghat.*

A prince happened to be fishing just near about there at the time. He noticed that a beautiful maiden got out of the fruit and bathed in the river. She was so beautiful that she made the whole neighbourhood bright with her presence. Having dried her hair in the sun, she re-entered the *ow* and rolled back to her mother.

The prince was charmed with the beauty of the maiden. He left his fishing-rod then and there, and returning to his father's palace hastened to the *Roh-ghar* † and shut himself up there. His parents looked for him high and low, but could find him nowhere. At last they found him lying disconsolate in that room. On being asked what the matter was with him, he said that he must marry the rolling *ow* of the house of such and such a king. At first both the king and the queen tried to console the prince and said that it was an impossibility—the whole

* Ghat is a place where there are steps and passage to get into the water.

† A room in which a member of a Royal family shuts himself or herself up when in sorrow or in a temper.

idea was absurd and ridiculous, but the prince was obdurate. His father could not dissuade him from his purpose. He, therefore, with great reluctance sent a formal proposal for the marriage of the *ow* with the prince. The fruit's mother began to shed bitter tears thinking that they were ridiculing her. At last, however, not being able to resist the king's importunities, she cleaned and washed the *ow* and gave it in marriage with the prince The ceremony was performed in the manner of all royal marriages and the prince brought his bride home.

After finishing his dinner at night the prince shared the same bedroom with the *ow*. He was wont to leave a portion of the meal sent him by his mother. When the prince used to fall asleep, the *ow-maiden* would come out of the *ow*, eat the food thus left and re-enter it. In the morning when the prince used to be awakened from his sleep, not a single morsel of food would he find left on the plate This made him very depressed and thoughtful, as he could not fathom this mystery.

One day a beggar woman came to beg a handful of rice from the prince. Seeing him in such depression she said, "My child, I find you sitting very morose, why so? You have brought

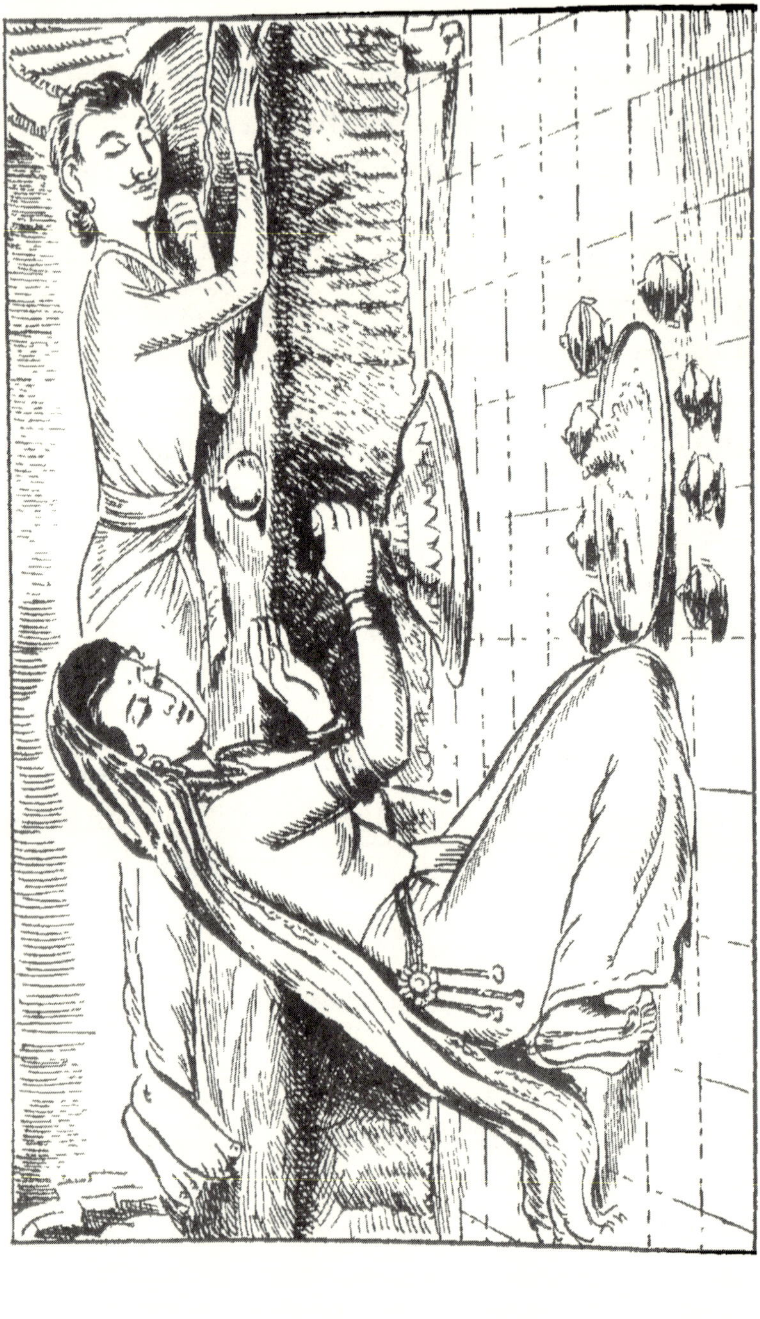

a wife home—how is it that we have not seen her, for she is our daughter you know?" Hearing the gentle tone of the beggar woman the prince unburdened himself of his sorrow and related the whole story of his marriage to her. The old woman said, "*Bapa* (my child), it is your own princess who is inside the *ow*. Listen therefore and I will counsel you. Burn a bright fire with paddy-husk in your bed-room to-night and have near by a bowlful of rice well mixed with *athia* banana and curd. Go to your bed and begin to snore and pretend as if you are sound asleep When the maiden would emerge from her shell to satisfy her hunger, get up at once and thrust the fruit into the fire. But then you will find that the maiden would suddenly faint and fall to the ground You will then take some of the paste with rice, curd and banana and bandage her head with it; she will then come round in no time" Pleased with the advice of the beggar woman he rewarded her handsomely He followed her instructions the same night, and became the proud possessor of the *ow-maiden*.

The next morning when the king and the queen were informed of this incident they were beside themselves with joy and hastily sent word to the other king and queen. They were all happy at this termination of this curious union and both the prince and the princess were married again in all becoming pomp and splendour.

The Jungle Crow and The Wren

(Dhora Kauri Aru Tipachi Charai)

Once upon a time there were a jungle crow and a little wren bird They made friends. One day when they were perched on a tree they saw an old woman drying some boiled rice in the sun. The jungle crow said to the little bird, "Friend, friend, do you see the old woman drying her boiled rice in the sun—let us go and get some." The little bird said, "Yes, let us" "My friend," replied the jungle crow, "but there is a condition ; if you can't carry as much rice in your beak as I shall in mine, I shall eat you up, and if I can't carry as much in mine as you will in yours, you will eat me up." These words made the little bird think that it was impossible that she would be able to carry as much as the jungle crow ; and so she came to the conclusion that it was the jungle crow's intention to eat her. But she said to herself, "Let me see however, how he does it" and she replied, "Very well, friend, I am game." The jungle crow then said to the little bird, "Have your chance first, then." The wren replied, "No friend, you had better have yours first," on which the jungle crow replied, "No friend, it is you who are to have your turn, first I come after you The wren on hearing this brought a beakful with her little beak. The jungle crow followed after and he brought many times as much with his beak as the little bird brought in hers. And the jungle crow then said, "Friend, let me now eat you up" "Certainly, you will eat me up" said the wren, "but you see you eat all manner of dead bodies and your beak has an awful smell. Pray, go and wash your beak in the sea and then come and eat me up." The jungle crow replied, "Very well, friend, I shall do just as you ask me to and return immediately after I have washed it in the sea." And he flew to the sea and called out, "Brother Sea, Brother Sea." The sea replied, "What is it ?" The jungle crow said, "Give me some water to wash my beak. For I want to eat a wren chick." The sea replied, "How shall I give it to you ? If you can bring with you some sort of cup, bowl, or a jar I may give you some then, how otherwise ?'

The jungle crow on hearing this flew to a potter to get a jar On reaching the potter's he called out, "Brother Potter, Brother Potter, are you at home ?" The potter replied, "Yes, what can I do for you ?" The jungle crow said, "Give me a jar so that I may have some water to wash my beak with and eat a little wren " The potter said, "I have not any jar ready at present If you get me a little clay, I could make you one "

Then the jungle crow went and asked for some clay from the earth saying, "Give me some clay so that I may give it to the potter to make a jar to draw some water. I wish to wash my beak and eat a little wren " The earth replied, "How can I help you with some myself ? If you can manage to dig some, you are welcome,"

On having this reply the jungle crow hastened to a buffalo and said, "Lend me your horn to dig the earth with. I want to take it over to the potter for a jar. I shall then draw some water to wash my beak with and eat the wren."

The buffalo replied, "How can I give you my horn myself ? If you can manage to take it, do

so." Whereupon the jungle crow approached a dog and said, "Kill the buffalo, I want his horn to dig the clay with so that I may give it to a potter to make me a jar to draw water in to wash my beak with and eat the wren."

The dog replied, "I have not had milk for a long time. so I am not as strong as I was. If you can get me some milk, I shall be able to kill the baffalo."

On hearing this the jungle crow approached a cow and said, "Give me milk to feed the dog who will kill the buffalo for me and give me his horn I shall dig the earth with it and give it to the potter to make me a jar with which I shall draw water to wash my beak and then eat the wren." The cow replied, "I am getting old now ; I have not had a good feed of grass for a long time ; if you can get me some good grass I shall give you as much milk as you like."

Then the jungle crow addressed the grass saying, "Give me some grass to feed the cow who would give me milk for the dog who would kill the buffalo, etc. etc"

The grass replied, "How could I give you some myself ? You are welcome to cut and take it,"

He then went to the blacksmith and called

out from outside, "Brother Smith, are you in?" The blacksmith replied, "Yes, Brother Crow, what brings you here?" The jungle crow replied, "Give me a spade, I want to cut some grass to feed the cow, etc. etc."

The blacksmith said, "The fire has gone out, if you can get some fire I shall make you a spade most gladly"

The jungle crow happening to look round saw some smoke on the other side of the water. No sooner he saw it than he flew to the other side and found an old woman boiling some paddy. He approached her and asked for some fire. The old woman said, "How will you carry it?" The jungle crow replied, "Well, tie some to my wing"

The old woman did so. The jungle crow crossed the sea and when he was flying across, the wind blowing hard, the wings caught fire and he dropped on to the water and was drowned.

And now the wren was all along noticing what the jungle crow was doing from beginning to end. He, on witnessing such an end of the jungle crow, flew away in great delight from his perch to a branch of another tree

I too, had to return as my clothes had to be sent to be washed.

The fern opened out its ear and my tale has come to an end. The areca-nut has opened its flower ; who will go where ? The black cat's white ears , call out the name of Rama.*

A Flower-Maiden And A Flower Plant

(Ejani Malinee Aru Ejopa Phool)

Once upon a time there was a *Malinee* or female gardener and she planted a flower-plant with great care Though she used to look after it with great care yet it would not flower. She therefore asked it one day, "Plant, Plant, why do you not flower ?" The plant replied, "If I am to

* The narrator of every Assamese tale ends his tale with such meaningless words in rhyme. This is somewhat like "The Natiya tree withereth" of Rev. Lal Bihary Day's *Folk Tales of Bengal.* To give it a semblance of truth as if he had been present there he also winds up his tale with such words as "I had to come back, etc"

flower, why then does the cow eat my shoot ?" The *Malinee* thereupon approached the cow and asked, "Cow, Cow, why is it that you eat the shoot of the plant ?"

Cow : Why doesn't the cowherd look after me and why should not I then eat the shoot ?

Malinee · Cowherd, Cowherd, why don't you mind the cow ?

Cowherd : The cook does not give me rice, why should I then mind her ?

Malinee : Cook, Cook, why do you not give rice to the cowherd ?

Cook : Why does not the faggot-seller give faggots, how else could I give rice ?

Malinee : Faggot-seller, Faggot-seller, why don't you give faggots ?

Faggot-seller : The blacksmith does not give me an axe, how could I then give ?

Malinee : Blacksmith, Blacksmith, why do you not give an axe ?

Blacksmith . The charcoal-seller does not give me any charcoal, how could I give an axe ?

Malinee : Charcoal-seller, Charcoal-seller, why do you not give charcoal ?

Charcoal-seller : If I am to give charcoal, why does the cloud shower rain ?

Malinee : Cloud, Cloud, why do you shower rain ?

Cloud : Why does then the frog croak ?

Malinee . Frog, Frog, why do you croak ?

Frog · Why should I give up the practice of my ancestors ?

The Tale of a Cunning Fox

(*Budhiak Shial*)

One night a fox was stealthily peering into every house and garden of a village looking for some food to satisfy his hunger. While doing so he found in the storeroom of a certain house some cakes dedicated to the goddess Lakshmi.

They were in a brass vessel with a hole at its bottom. He, fox-like, devoured all the cakes and while licking off with great gusto the little bits left over on the banana-leaf placed there to cover over the hole of the vessel it got fixed round his neck like a neck-ring. He tried his best to get himself out of this awkward situation but did not succeed.

The poor fox was now unable to purloin a duck or a goat even, for no sooner he emerged from the forest the vessel made a noise which warned the people who would then start chasing him shouting—"Catch the neck-ring, catch the neck-ring !"

One day while he was aimlessly wandering about the forest he came across a couple of tiger cubs with some meat in front of them. And he immediately devised a means to partake of it. Making a great deal of noise by shaking the vessel about with his head he called out from a distance, "Well, where have your parents gone

ot, young'uns ? I suppose they have run away in fear of me as soon as they heard me Now then, say at once where they are" The two little tiger cubs frightened at the commanding and awe-inspiring voice of the fox said in gentle tones, "Sir, our parents have gone out in search of game" The fox replied, "Well, never mind, tell them I called, as soon as they return Look here, your father borrowed this vesselful of money from me years and years ago, he has not repaid it as yet. I can't wait long ; to-day as he returns tell him about this, will you? I am hungry, let me have something to eat if there is anything about" The fox then devoured the meat left by their parents for the cubs and departed

It became the daily programme of the fox to put in an appearance and eat up the food left for the cubs whenever the tigers were out hunting. This continued for a long time and the cubs began to get thinner It set the mother a-thinking; why are the little mites getting so thin? Does anyone do them out of the meat we leave behind for them? Thinking thus she addressed her mate, "Listen, you need not go out hunting to-day—I had better go alone. It is time that we saw if anybody came here in our absence. Keep yourself concealed here to-day and watch attentively." Leaving the tiger behind, the tigress set out alone.

As was his practice the fox appeared before the cubs shaking the vessel. As soon as the tiger saw that the fox was arranging to eat the meat up he set upon him with a terrific roar and ran after him, The cunning fox had foreseen it and had made out his plan of escape from before. He therefore continued to run and slipped through an opening of a tree between two branches The tiger in trying to get through the same opening got himself caught and squeezed between them He did his best to extricate himself but his every effort to get

out entangled him all the more The whole forest rang with his terrific roar and all other animals began to flee in fear. His roars brought the tigress to the spot The fox was chuckling over the tiger's difficulty at a little distance, and as soon as he saw her he began to bawl out, "Do you see now, the difficulty your husband is in, how I have pinned him? You were jolly eager to borrow money and did not care a rap whether you repaid or not. Well, I will serve you the same way if you don't repay me without delay. If you can't repay, well, I won't be hard with you—if you can't pay me at once you must obey me and do as I tell you. If you don't do it, rest assured, there would be no quarters for you. And I swear there will be an end of your dear little mites too."

After struggling hard in vain to make good his escape the tiger expired. And seeing no other means of escape from the clutches of the fox the tigress became entirely subservient to him. Now the fox began to enjoy himself thoroughly He used to send the tigress out hunting and himself sit at home and eat to his heart's content as he did never in his life before.

Some time after this came the season for the tigress to change her den. She with her two little cubs, was making preparations for getting across to the forest on the other side of the river when the fox too joined them. The tigress with her cubs started crossing the river and willy nilly, the fox too to keep his self-respect and prestige as their guardian started, not caring a jot what would happen to him. He was about to be carried away by the strong current of the water and when he was floundering and looking as if he would sink, the tigress, seeing his distress, clutched him and swam across to the other side safely with him. As soon as he found himself safe and sound on land he started swaggeringly telling her, "Why on earth did you bring me from the water ? Who asked you to do so ? You females are senseless, you have not an atom of sense. The fact of the matter is, the river-god owes me four vesselfuls of money and whenever he sees me he avoids me. But I had the better of him to-day and I thought I would not leave him till our account was settled, when you came and unfortunately intervened in the matter Why did you ? We were just having a tussle and you spoilt everything. Why did you do it—eh ? Tell me now ? Will you ?" These growls settled the tigress and he continued domineering over her just as before

The two little cubs came to their years of discretion and started hunting on their own. The tigers and the fox took to hunt by turns Of course as you would guess the fox tried to avoid it as much as possible with his usual skill and cunning. One day, however, he was obliged to accompany the tigress on her hunt. He said to her, "I shall lie in wait for him here, and you had better drive the deer round my way and I will manage the rest." And accordingly the tigress chased the deer away towards where the fox was lying in wait. The deer however not minding him a bit trod on him and ran away. His skin was considerably mangled by the tread. When the tigress came up to him he said, "Look here, as soon as the deer came running this way I could not for the life of me refrain from laughing. Could one like me kill such a small thing as that deer? I laughed and laughed till I actually burst with laughing"

This time too the fox scored a victory and he continued to lord it over them all. The two cubs after a time became aware of his tricks and they planned among themselves to expose him. One night when other foxes were having their usual nocturnal concert he too felt tempted to join in it and he stealthily went some distance for that purpose not knowing that he was closely watched and followed by the cubs. And when he found himself at a safe distance, as he thought, he started bellowing to his heart's content. Now the cubs were sure of his identity and as soon as they found out that he was only a fox after all, they caught hold of him and tore him to pieces.

The Tale Of The Tiger And The Crab

(*Bagh Aru Kekorar Sadhu*)

Long long ago there lived a tiger. He came across a crab on the way when he was removing from one den to another. The crab addressed him with a smile, "Brother, where are you going ?" The tiger pleased with the beaming face of the crab replied, "I am removing from one den to another. Where may you be going ?" The crab replied, "I am going nowhere, I live close by, I am all alone in the world, I have none to look to." The tiger rejoined, "I am in the same way myself, I too am all alone in the world, helpless and friendless." And after a conversation of this nature they became friends and settled to live near each other in that forest.

Thus they lived in peace and amity for some time. The tiger used to hunt deer and have a fair division both for himself as well as for the crab. All other wild animals used to keep at a respectful distance from the crab and would not molest him in any way as they were afraid of the tiger. One day the crab told the tiger,

"Friend, I am tired of taking meat every day—well, to tell you the truth my digestion is getting to be badly affected—what do you say to a pure

vegetarian repast now and then? Let us turn cultivators." The tiger responded, "There is no difficulty in the matter. If you like it, come along, let us do it." Then the crab proposed that the tiger should go to the village and get some small rice plants, (which are ready for transplanting into other fields for growing) and he himself had better see about ploughing the plot of field close by. And the crab started ploughing the land assisted by the tiger who carried away nice little *manikimadhuri** rice seedlings and planted them on it After a time the rice plants began to bloom with paddy. Naturally they were quite elated over the result and the crab then said, "Now that we have earned some rice we must have some vegetables with it We can't eat only rice you know Let us then try and see if we can grow some vegatables on this plot of land close by. You had better go, friend, to the village and get vegetable seedlings of various sorts and don't you forget a few brinjal plants. I shall in the meantime start ploughing this plot here." And the crab started ploughing, but no sooner had the tiger gone a few paces than the crab called out, "Friend, I had quite forgotten about chilli—don't you forget to bring some chilli

* An excellent quality of sweet-scented rice.

plants. It goes very well with acid curry." The tiger then started on his errand with long strides.

Gradually the month of Aghon approched —and the paddy was ripe for cutting. After making the necessary arrangements for reaping the corn, the tiger asked the crab, "Friend, will you take the top end or the bottom end ?" The crab was quite cute and he said he would have the top end. He therefore had the top end that is to say, the real paddy and the tiger had the stubble. Then the time approached for plucking the aubergines, and the tiger asked the crab, "Friend, which will you have, the seed or the plants ?" The crab replied he would have the seed, and he had the brinjals while the plants were left for the tiger. When they had gathered all the field-produce together, each his own share, the tiger invited the crab to dinner one day. He cooked the stubble and the brinjal plants as well as he could, but how could the crab eat all that ? He just made a pretence of eating and departed. Be that as it may, even after this he used to have full course meat-breakfasts and dinners with the tiger. He never returned the compliment by asking the tiger to have any meal with him. The tiger felt it and said, "Friend, you have never asked me to dine with you. I should like to have a taste of your dishes —they must be well-cooked." "My dear friend," the crab replied, "I have been thinking of asking you to dinner for a long time, but you know, old fellow, I am rather hard up for space in my digs and thinking that I could not honour you sufficiently I have not done so If you would however not take anything amiss but take me as I am, I shall be so pleased if you will come and take pot luck with me to-morrow morning." "Right gladly will I do it, my friend, I shall certainly turn up to-morrow morning."

The next morning the crab boiled his *manikimadhuri* rice and cooked a deliciously tasty curry with brinjals. When the tiger came the crab welcomed him and said, "Friend, be you seated at the entrance outside, for you know I am cramped for space here Make yourself at home and eat as much as you like" The crab began to serve out dishes and the tiger started his meal. The cooking utensils the crab had were small and whatever was cooked in them the tiger finished up in two mouthfuls He then grew frightened and said to himself, "There is no trusting a tiger. If he is not satisfied with the meal he would think nothing of eating me up forgetting all about our friendship." And he contrived a plan and said, "Friend, I am afraid I have got quite tired of coming up and down with the dinner like this, as a matter of fact I have a pain at the back. You had better put your tail into the hole, and I shall tie the dishes on to it and you will take them out and eat to your heart's content leisurely". The tiger did not see through it and did as he was told. And as soon as he did it, the crab squeezed the tail so hard, that he could not extricate himself ; and the more he tried to extricate himself the more he got squeezed. The poor tiger began to roar with all his might, but the crab would not let go his tail. Fortunately the tiger saw a farmer (the only son of a widow) hoeing not very far. He was about to run away in fear, when the tiger began to entreat and beseech him to help him to get out the tail. The farmer said, "I can't do it, you are a tiger, there's no trusting you, and as soon as I help you to get out your tail, you will eat me up." The tiger said, "My father, come, do. I solemnly swear I will not eat you ,—come and get me out of this hole. If you save me from this danger then I assure you I will get you a deer every day." On hearing this assurance, the farmer grew bold and approaching the tiger, chopped his tail off. The tiger thanked him and whispered, "I will get you a deer everyday to be sure, but don't you tell it to anybody ; if you do, wherever you may be at the time, I will carry you off from there."

And the tiger was true to his word and supplied him with a deer every day. After some time the farmer fell ill, and his mother sent for an old fortune-telling woman who after her calculations told her that her son would recover if a feast were given to their friends and relatives. So the mother told her son of it, and he ordered the tiger to bring two deer for the feast, which he did.

On the day of the feast, when everyone was seated, each in his seat, it was found that they were short by one banana leaf, and one of the guests went to the garden to get a leaf. While there, he saw a number of bones all in a heap as high as a small hill, and without cutting off a leaf from the plant, he came back and told the assembled guests, "Friends, we cannot dine in this house, as our host seems to eat some forbidden food. Please come and judge for yourselves, or how could he come by such a heap of bones ?" They did not eat when they went to the place and found that what their fellow guest had told them was indeed too true.

They then told the widow's son that unless he told them what bones they were they would not touch a morsel there. He replied, "Gentlemen, have my assurance that the animals whose bones you see there are not forbidden for food by the *Shastras* But I am sorry to say, I am not in a position to tell you anything more about it in detail—if I do it the tiger will carry me off." The guests said, "Never you mind, we will surround you with spears and lances carefully Tell us, unless you do, we won't touch anything here." Seeing no way out of it, the farmer knelt down and began to narrate the tale while every one there protected him surrounding him with spears and lances. As soon as he had finished his tale, the tiger sprang upon him from no one knew where and carried him off. The guests were much confounded at this and looked for him for a little while. They searched for him in vain and went away.

The tiger, in the meantime, carried the boy to a dense forest. As good luck would have it the boy felt hungry and his stomach began to rumble. The tiger asked him, "What is that rumbling in your stomach?" The farmer boy felt his wits returning to him and said, "When I was a little boy my mother had given me one hundred and twenty crabs to eat ;—three score of the lot came out long ago, and the remaining three score will soon be out now." The tiger at the mere mention of 'crabs' shrank in terror ; —he thought one crab was about to do for him, and what would not these three score do ! He left the farmer in the forest then and there, and ran for his very life.

Having thus save himself from the clutches of the tiger, he found his way to a river and rested under a tree near it He noticed that wild buffaloes herded under that tree and he drank off what little milk there was left on the ground, and sweeping the place quite clean, mounted the tree for the night.

When the buffaloes returned in the evening, they were quite surprised to find the place swept so clean. They searched everywhere but could find no one, and they wondered who that person could be who cleaned the place. The next day when the buffaloes went for pasture, the farmer climbed down the tree and drank whatever little milk was left on the ground and swept the place clean with cowdung and lodged up in the tree for the night as before. On their return, the buffaloes were surprised again to find that the place was kept so clean. When they went for pasture the next day, they left an old buffalo behind them with instructions to keep a look out for the mysterious individual, telling him that they would bring back a lot of grass and drink for him. But the old buffalo fell asleep at noon on account of the heat, and the farmer came down and quietly did the same as before. The old buffalo saw or heard nothing.

When they returned in the evening, they questioned the old buffalo but he had seen nothing. The next day they thought the buffalo was getting old, and he was good for nothing. Instead of him therefore, they left an one-eyed buffalo to keep guard the next day. This buffalo kept his sound eye down and fell asleep. The farmer did the same that day too and the buffalo knew nothing of it.

Then their leader took it upon himself to keep guard the next day. During the day once he fell asleep and the farmer finding his opportunity came down and did as before. But as soon as he climbed the tree the leader opened his eyes and saw him. "Are you a god or a man? Answer me. Be you god or man, come down," said the leader. The farmer replied, "I am not a god but a man and I am afraid of coming down, as you will gore me to death." The leader said, "No, I won't." Then the buffalo took three oaths that he was speaking the truth, and he would never gore him. Being assured thereby, he came down and related the whole story to him. The buffalo took pity on him, and said that he would be the master of the whole herd and there would be a buffalo specially reserved for him to supply him with milk When the rest of the buffaloes returned, they were informed of it all, and they each and one acknowledged him as their master. They then killed the one-eyed buffalo and supplied him with her two horns They named one of them as the merry-horn and the other as the angry-horn If the merry-horn were blown by the farmer boy, and they happened to be away, they would conclude that he was happy and well and they would then graze with ease and without care, but if the angry-horn were to be blown, they would conclude that he was in distress and they would all run for his protection. In return for all this, he was to sweep clean the place as heretofore.

They lived thus happily for a long time. One day when the young man was combing his hair one of his good flowing hairs dropped into the river and it was devoured by a *raghoborali* fish After a time a fisherman caught the fish and thinking that the king would be pleased with it he made a present of it to him.

This king had a young and lovely daughter. She happened to be present at the time when the fish was being prepared for the kitchen by the maids. Seeing such a lovely flowing hair inside the fish, she took it from the maids and accepted its owner in her mind as her lord and master. She then placed it carefully in a small case and locked herself in a "grieving" room of the palace. When the king inquired why she had thus locked harself in, she replied that unless and until the owner of that hair was found and married to her she would eat and drink nothing and would starve herself to death. The king was thunderstruck on hearing this. How was he to find out when and where the fish swallowed that hair and who its owner was ! It was an utter impossibility and the king was quite at sea as to how to find it out. Find it out however he must, or his daughter would die.

The princess had a pet jungle crow. And he approached the king and begged him not to grieve any longer, as he would find out who the owner of the hair was ; only he had to be given a ripe mango. The king was much relieved to hear this and got him a ripe mango. The jungle crow flew with it to the forest where the farmer boy was, and he sang out, "Who is it that blows the merry-horn and the angry-horn and who wants to eat a ripe mango?"

The farmer boy on hearing about the mango, felt tempted and responded, "It is I who blow the merry-horn and the angry-horn and I should like to eat the ripe mango il I get it." The jungle crow then gave it to the farmer boy, but as soon as he stretched his hand to take the mango the jungle crow flew away with the angry-horn. Do you see, how the jungle crow did the farmer boy in the eye? Isn't there a saying that the crow is the cunningest of all birds! Bereft of the angry-horn the farmer boy was helpless and he began to blow the merry-horn with all his might. The buffaloes concluded on hearing the merry-horn so often that their master was happy and they grazed in peace.

The jungle crow went back in triumph to the king and handing him the angry-horn said, "I know who the owner of that hair is. The same person owns this horn too—and now if your Majesty would allow a few officers to come with me I would show him to them." It was easy now to get at the boy as he had not the angry-

horn. The king's officers placed him before the king. When he was being carried away, the farmer boy tore his clothes into pieces and left a trace behind him all along the route. When the buffaloes returned in the evening, they, on not finding their master in his place, concluded that some evil had befallen him. They followed the track of torn shreds of cloth left behind by their master and found themselves in the presence of the king. On seeing such a large number of buffaloes, the king grew frightened and the boy said that the whole herd was his own. On seeing their master again, the buffaloes were frantic with joy. When the king heard this, he said, "If they are your buffaloes can you, without any danger to yourself, mount on one and leap from one to another ?" The farmer boy did this at once and the king finding that what the boy had said was true, then and there arranged for the princess's marriage with him. The son-in-law was then made the reigning monarch while the king remained a monarch only in name.

We had to return, for our clothes had to be sent to the wash.

Tejimola

Once upon a time there lived a merchant who had two wives. The elder one had only one child, a daughter, Tejimola by name. The younger one had no issue. Tejimola's mother died when she was yet a child and her step-mother therefore brought her up. She, being the only child in the house, was a great favourite with her father. The step-mother however in her heart of hearts detested her—the fear of her husband's anger and displeasure only made her look after and take care of the child.

The child grew in the meantime and when she became about ten or eleven years of age, her father got her to make friends with the daughter of a well-to-do man of the village, a girl of the same age as herself.

Tejimola's father could not do without merchandise, and business took him about from place to place. He had on one occasion to go out on business for about six or seven months, When the time came for him to depart, he called his wife to him and bade her look after the child during his absence, saying, "Now that I have to go on business, I am leaving Tejimola entirely in your hands. Do look after her, love her and tend her carefully, the dear little child."

The merchant's wife thought that this was her opportunity, and she could do as she liked with her and could ill-treat her to her heart's content. She then, on second thoughts, said to herself that it would not be wise merely to stop at ill-treating and beating her, for she must somehow or other find some means of doing away with her altogether—for she was but her stepdaughter and at the time of her marriage her father would give her a large dowry, perhaps of jewellery and furniture much cherished and stored so long by her—why should her step-daughter get the advantage of those things? She might just as well send the things home to her mother: It was better to do away with her altogether. From that very day, the day when her husband's boat left the village, she was looking for some loophole or other in the child's conduct to chastise her, and actually did cause the poor girl to suffer for nothing on the slightest pretence.

And now her friend's wedding was approaching—it was to take place the day after. Tejimola's greatest desire was to assist at the wedding and to stay with her friend for three or four days during the marriage festivities. Her friend too was very anxious that she should do so.

Now the step-mother saw that her long-looked for chance had come and gave her permission to go to the wedding. She made a great fuss and showed a great deal of concern on behalf of the girl, and discussed before a number of people what dresses Tejimola should wear during the festivities, whether this *riha** would go well with this *mekhela* and whether she should wear that other sort of *mekhela* with that *riha*. She had a lovely silk *riha* and fine silk *mekhela* and a gold-embroidered *khonia* wrapper—at last she brought them out and said to her, "My dear, wear these when you are at your friend's house. I had better make them up into a parcel. You go as you are now and wear these just as you are about to reach your friend's place. If you were to wear them now they would get soiled and would not be worth wearing them." And she secretly put a mouse in between the *riha* and the *mekhela* and some embers in the *khonia* and packing them all up into a dainty parcel handed them over to Tejimola.

Riha, breast-cloth, *mekhela*, lower garment, skirt-like.

Just as she was about to reach her friend's house, she unpacked the parcel, but lo and behold, a mouse sprang out from the *riha* and *mekhela* and some burnt ashes dropped from the *khonia*! And there was consternation in her face when she found that the mouse had torn the *riha* and the *mekhela* into shreds and the gold embroidered wrapper was burnt into many holes. She was frightened almost to death, and she began to quake in fear and sob aloud The attendant, who was with her, was also very much surprised at this, and he tried his best to console her. He got her a pair of *riha* and *mekhela* from her friend's house and she managed to witness and enjoy the festivities with that dress On her return home after the wedding, when the step-mother asked for her clothes she quaked with fear and dropped the torn and burnt clothes before her. The step-mother made a pretence of being very angry at it and abused and thrashed her almost to death. Yet the mother was not satisfied. She dragged poor Tejimola to the rice and paddy pounding apparatus. She then asked her to supply the paddy in the hole and she began to pound away with all her might. As she was doing it the step-mother all of a sudden pressed the instrument hard on her right hand which

crushed it completely. Poor Tejimola shrieked in pain at this, and the relentless step-mother beginning to strike her with a broom ordered her to do her work with her left hand. As the unfortunate girl was doing her work with her left hand that too was crushed in the same manner as the right. Then the step-mother ordered her to do it with her right foot which received the same treatment as her hands—then the left foot was served the same way. The head only remained and she was asked to do the work with her head That too was crushed—and then poor Tejimola died.

Having thus killed the unfortunate girl who was her father's darling, she buried her secretly just under the eaves of the rice-pounding shed.

After some time a beautiful little pumpkin plant grew on the spot where she was buried. The plant was full of lovely big pumpkins. Not seeing Tejimola about for a long time the neighbours questioned the step-mother about her, who promptly replied that Tejimola had not yet returned from her friend's wedding.

A beggar woman came one day and begged a pumpkin from the merchant's wife. She was surprised on hearing this strange request for she had no pumpkin in her garden. She had not the courage to go near the spot where Tejimola was buried since that incident and consequently had not seen the pumpkin plant gradually creeping over the roof ; so she said, "My good woman, where could I get a pumpkin ? I have not had one for an age myself." The beggar woman replied, "Why, mother, there is a beautiful plant creeping over the roof of your rice pounding shed with some lovely pumpkins."

The merchant's wife was taken aback and she replied, "If there be a pumpkin plant certainly take by all means as many pumpkins as you like."

The beggar woman then went to the spot and no sooner she did so than the pumpkin plant sang out plaintively :—

"Stretch not thy hands nor pluck a pumpkin—thou strange beggar woman, my step-mother did crush me for the silk cloths and it is I, Tejimola"

The beggar woman got terribly frightened on hearing a pumpkin plant sing and she came back to the merchant's wife and said, "Mother, when I went to pluck a pumpkin the plant began to sing out—I don't want any pumpkin, madam, I am off." And she left. The merchant's wife understood what it was and went with a knife to the spot and cut the plant off, root and all, and threw it away in a remote corner of her garden.

Just on the spot where the pumpkin plant was thrown away there grew a shaddock tree. It was loaded with fruits so much so that some of the branches touched the ground. Some cow-herd boys not being able to resist the temptation, approached the merchant's wife and asked her for some of the fruits. She replied that she had no such tree in the orchard ; but the boys said that they had seen a tree full of fruits just at a remote corner in the garden. She then said they were welcome to them if they could find them. Rejoiced with their success they went to the spot ; but as they were about to pluck the fruits the tree began plaintively to sing :—

"Oh, my brothers dear, cowherd boys of the village, neither stretch your hand nor pluck the fruits—return home—it is, I, Tejimola who am buried here crushed to death by my step-mother."

The boys, hearing this plaintive strain, thought that the tree was haunted and being frightened left the spot at once. They came to the merchant's wife and told her all about it. When it struck her that it was just there where she had thrown the pumpkin plant, she came to the conclusion that it was Tejimola who was there as a shaddock tree. She went to the spot and up-rooted it completely aud threw it into the river.

The shaddock plant floated along the river and in one of its shallow pools it rested as a lovely water-lily. Sometime later the merchant was returning home that way and seeing the lovely lily wanted to take it home for his dear daughter Tejimola. He directed his oarsmen to take the boat to the spot and asked one of them to pluck the lily. When the boatman was going to pluck it the lily began, as before, to sing plaintively. The boatman became terrified and would not pluck it. This made the merchant curious and he went to pluck it himself. The lily then began to sing out, "Father dear, neither stretch your hands nor pluck the lily. It is I, Tejimola who was crushed to death by my step-mother only for the silk cloths."

The father was quite aware of his wife's conduct and behaviour towards his daughter, so he thought it must be his own Tejimola. To find out whether it was so or not he took out some areca from his mouth which he was then chewing. He placed it on his left hand and on his right he took a sweet (laddoo) and he said, "If you be really my own Tejimola you will appear as a *myna* and chew the the areca on my left hand ; but if you are anybody else, you will take this sweet on my right hand." The lily at once was transformed into a *myna* and perching itself on his left hand chewed the areca. The merchant was sure then that it was his own Tejimola and bringing a cage put the *myna* in it.

When he reached home he asked his wife where Tejimola was. She said that she had gone to her uncle's place ; but the husband began to put her question after question which brought out the truth. Then the merchant threw his *gamocha** on the *myna* and said, "If you are really my Tejimola and love me, you will take your human shape at once and wear this *gamocha*." Tejimola then regained her human form.

The merchant drove his wife away from his home.

---

* *Gamocha* literally means something with which one wipes one's person, a towel.

The Old Man, The Old Woman And The Fox

(*Burha, Burhi Aru Shial*)

Once upon a time there was an old man and his old woman. One day when the old man was about to plant some arum tubers, some foxes came and said to him, "Grandfather, are you planting the arum raw or cooked ?" The old man replied "My sons, I am planting them raw." They then said, "Grandfather, we are afraid you are not following the right method. You had better boil them first and then dig holes where you will plant them. After that is done put some straw at the bottom and then place some areca-nut bark on the straw. After you have done that you will plant the arum, not before ; cover them over with straw afterwards. If you follow this method you will find that the arum will grow big in one night." And the old man replied, "Alright my sons, I will follow your advice."

He boiled all the arum in the evening and planted them according to their advice. At night the foxes had a grand time of it and ate them all. When the old man went to look at the plants the next morning he was very much ashamed of himself to find that he was taken in by the foxes in that manner.

Sometime after this incident the old man asked the old woman to rub some treacle on his person saying, "As soon as the flies will come trooping round me to feed on the treacle you will start wailing and when the foxes will come to inquire what is up, you will tell them that I was dead and you will then ask them to take me out and eat me. But keep a good-sized stick by me and as soon as they will come in to carry me away you will shut the door at once. I shall then rise immediately and beat them to death with the stick." The old woman having followed the old man's advice, the foxes came to her and asked, "Grandmother, why are you crying? What is the matter with you?" She replied, "My sons, my old man is dead and that is why I am weeping. If you can manage it, take him out and eat him." On hearing this they entered the room in great glee and no sooner they did this, she shut the door. The old man then got up at once and beat them all to death except four who somehow or other managed to make good their escape.

Sometime after this the old woman told her husband that she had all this time been indoors for fear of the foxes and being quite freed of this she had made up her mind to go and see her daughter. The old man advised her not to venture out, as finding her quite alone they were sure to molest her. She had however made up her mind to go and go she must. And she went. Finding her all alone on the way the foxes surrounded her and dancing around her said, "Now, you old woman, we won't let you go, we will eat you up." The old woman replied, "Well, my sons, if you will eat me up, well then you will, but you see I have not seen my dear daughter for a long time and I should just like to see her once before I die ; let me come back—you will then be quite welcome to eat me up." They replied, "Supposing you didn't come back ?" She said, "Is it likely that I should not come back to my dear husband, my children ? I take my oath I will return this very same way and you will then do just as you wish with me."

They then let her go aud she reached her daughter's house. She had a good time there as her daughter looked after her with great care and affection. When she told her daughter about her promise to the foxes, the latter suggested that she had a very big pumpkin-shell and her mother could easily get into it and roll along all the way to her village and the foxes would not know it And accordingly the old woman got into the shell and started rolling home. The foxes happened to see this curious and unique sight of a pumpkin rolling, and becoming suspicious they kicked and broke it to pieces. When the shell was broken they discovered that it was the old woman who was then trying to give them the slip and they were frantic with joy. They said, "Now then, old woman, you have been trying to give us the slip. You are caught now and what is to become of you ? We shall eat you now." She replied, "What can I do, my sons ? If you will eat me, why then you must ; but you see I have just learnt a very nice dance at my daughter's house. It is my great desire therefore to show you a few times how to do it. After I have done it—you are quite welcome to eat me." The foxes were sure of their victim and not being able to resist the temptation of seeing a new dance they agreed to her proposal. She said, "But you will have to do something—I shall sing as well as dance, you know, but when I start the tune, you will have to join in the chorus, that will make me dance all the better, boys."

I have forgotten to tell you that the old woman was discovered by the foxes not very far

from her house. The old woman then began to dance. She had a couple of dogs—*Ronga* (Reddie) and *Kola* (Blackie) by name. As she continued dancing, she sang out their names by turns which brought them to the spot. As soon as the foxes saw the dogs they took to their heels and our old woman reached home safely.

We too had to come away as we had to send our clothes to the wash.*

---

* All Assamese narrators of tales wind up with some such words to give the tale a semblance of truth, that is to say, to show that they were present during the incidents narrated in the tale.

The Long-Legged One

(Dighol-Thengiah)

Once upon a time there was an old woman and she eked out her livelihood somehow by selling milk from a few cows which she possessed. Her bed-room was very dilapidated—the thatch over her roof needed repairs sadly and the roof leaked. One rainy night as she was about to rest for the night after her meal, she prayed, "Oh, Lord, may the long-legged one not attack me," and she went to sleep.

It so happened that a thief was lurking near her cowshed waiting for her to retire with a view to robbing her of one of her cows. A tiger too was lying in wait in the darkness for her to retire with the same object in view. They both heard her prayer but, neither of them could make out what 'the long-legged one' meant.

She was just dozing off to sleep when the thief entered her cowshed. He began to think, "How could I in this darkness make out which cow is good or which is bad—the best test would, I think, be whichever cow jumps up as sŏon as

I touch her tail; she will be the sprightliest and best."

He then proceeded to feel the tails of each of them and when he unknowingly touched

the tiger's tail he jumped up all at once. The thief thought that that was the best of the lot and he had better take that one. He then started twisting the animal's tail with a view to driving it home, but as soon as he did so the tiger began to think that this was 'the long-legged one' of whom the old woman had muttered in her prayers. Being frightened, the tiger gave another jump. The thief thought that he could not manage this cow without mounting on the animal and as soon as he rode on the tiger the latter became thoroughly convinced that it was surely the "long-legged one" who had now got hold of him And he ran for all he was worth. The thief too came to the conclusion from the way the tiger was behaving, that it could not be a cow, but it must be "the long-legged one" of whom he had heard the old woman make mention. Each taking the other for the long-legged one they were both frantic with terror.

When the tiger was entering the forest with the thief on his back, he twisted his neck with all his might. It then struck the tiger that he could not be "the long-legged one" but he must be the neck-twister, The tiger then started running all the faster. The thief not being able to stop the tiger's progress by twisting his neck, caught hold of his tail again ; and as soon as the tiger felt the thief's hand on his tail it made him run all the more. The tiger was running so fast that the thief could no longer keep to his seat and fell down, but caught hold of his tail with such force that the tail came off in his hand. The tiger disappeared into the forest and after a few moment's consideration he came to the conclusion that it could not be the neck-twister even but he was surely the tailsnatcher,

The thief, on feeling the tail left in his hand, found out that it was not a cow's tail after all but a tiger's. He thereupon shook with fear It was then long before dawn and he therefore climbed a neighbouring mango-tree to spend the dreary night.

Now, the tiger related the whole of the awful tale to his brothers. A meeting was convened among them. They deliberated that it was a very shameful thing that such an event should have happened They were the leaders of the forest and that one of their brother leaders was thus put to ignominy and shame and insulted beyond description by a tail-snatcher it was impossible to endure Unless some steps were taken to remedy it, it would be a matter of great mortification and shame to their whole tribe. And besides if some other tribe of tailsnatchers were found to be stronger than they, they would then be no longer reckoned as leaders but will be classed among hewers of wood and drawers of water. Thus did they deliberate. And they came to the conclusion that they should all in a body start on an expedition without delay against this tail-snatcher

Nearly two score of tigers searched high and low for the tail-snatcher but nowhere could they

espy him. At last one of them happening to rest under the mango tree saw him comfortably ensconced on the tree. When he shouted that that was the tail-snatcher seated on the tree there was quite a commotion among them. They again put their heads together and made a plan as to how they would be able to get to him. They then began .to mount one upon the other, thus almost reaching the spot where the thief was seated. This made him naturally most uncomfortable and he thought that his end was not very far. Immediately however a good idea struck him. He saw that his friend the tailless tiger was seated last of all at the bottom end of the string of tigers. He then called out to him in an awe inspiring voice, "Look out, you tailless one, look out ! " This made the hapless tiger think that the tail-snatcher after all was making for him leaving all the others aside. When this thought occurred to him it filled him with great terror and he took to his heels running with all his might into the forest. This unlooked for move on the part of the brother warrior had the effect of tumbling all of them one after other, The other tigers not being able to fathom the cause of this incident,' came to the conclusion that they too were attacked by the tail-snatcher and ran in great fright for all they were worth to the forest.

The thief then passed the night on the tree and at day-break when he returned home he took a vow that he would never take to thieving again

---

The Globefish or Gangatope

One day all the fishes convened a meeting in the special corner of the river reserved for such meetings in order to discuss the ways and means of carrying on a campaign against all the fish-eaters. All sorts and conditions of fish from the *Row, Borali, Sole, Kawoi, Goroi,* and others to the very *Phool Dorikana* assembled in that meeting. After all the members had assembled, the company elected the bald-headed old *Goroi* as the president of the meeting and the sprightly *Chengeli* was elected the master of ceremonies He then requested Globefish *or Gangatope* to explain the objects of the meeting to the whole assembly Gangatope then with folded hands began his address ;—"Gentlemen and fellow subjects, having been blessed with the dust of your gracious feet and having been called upon by our worthy master of ceremonies Brother *Chengeli,* I am desirous of addressing a few words

to you. If in the course of my address to you I am guilty of any commissions or omissions, I look for your forgiveness and I hope you will forgive me on account of my tender age and lack of understanding. This is my humble prayer to you all.

"Of all the animals who are our enemies the animal who goes by the name of the "Man" is the worst. By means of fish-nets and other dangerous instruments of his making he catches us and throws us into the boiling oil or burning fire and eats us by various processes known as frying, grilling, boiling and in various other ways known to him alone. But please consider for a moment, gentlemen, though these men torture us and eat us in all these ways, they have after all been sent to this world by the Almighty as servants of all other animals. Go and look into the homes of these animals, you will see how they are slaving for such animals as the cows, the buffaloes, the horses, the goats and the others They supply grass to the cow and the horse, they find straw for them to sleep in, they build houses for them They even clean the dungs of all these animals.

"Fellow-subjects, if you come to consider the matter you will come to the conclusion that they must have been calves in days gone by, for they seem to be very fond of milk. It is seen among all animals and it is well known that they thrive on mother's milk. When you come to consider these things you cannot but come to the conclusion that they lack sadly in intelligence and are in no way better than cows. Therefore in my opinion we can finish such an animal as the Man merely by snapping our fingers.

'Fellow-subjects, I am a youth of tender age and am sadly lacking in intelligence ; therefore I have not been able to discuss fully all the points concerning our subject ot discussion to-day. I do not know why my aunt *Gedgedi* is not present in this meeting to-day. If she were present here she could have enlightened us more on the subject and could have told us in every detail how to do away with the most wretched of all animals—the Man. The reason why I say she could enlighten us more on the point is because she has a wider mouth. In days gone by it is said, my aunt *Gedgedi* with this same mouth swallowed one hundred crores of soldiers out of one hundred and eighty crores in the time of the battle of Kurukshetra. Let us therefore send for her at once so that she my testify to what I have said."

And the worthy president of the meeting the bald-heade Goroi ordered the master of ceremonies the sprightly Chengeli to go and fetch Mrs. Gedgedi forthwith. He sent a little Goroi to Mrs. Gedgedi's residence. Without a moment's delay the Goroi went to her residence as ordered and sang out, "Sister Gedgedi, Sister Gedgedi, will she go to the meeting or will she not ?"

On hearing these sing-song inquiries from

the Goroi the Gedgedi was angry beyond control and she snappishly replied, "Thou slave of a vain fellow ! Eater of your own offspring !—I won't go, go and tell them." On hearing this rude reply from her, brother Goroi went and reported the result of the interview to the meeting. The

Gangatope then himself volunteered to escort his aunt to the meeting and begged leave of the president therefore. Sister Gedgedi, though she had given such a rude reception to the Goroi-ling and had replied to his kind invitation so discourteously saying that she was not going, was nevertheless aware that she could not very well disobey the wishes of the assembly ; she therefore was about to leave for the meeting dressing herself with vermilion in proper manner when the Gangatope appeared on the scene. He called out, "Mother Kanchanmati, Mistress Gold, will she go to the meeting or will she not ?" The way the Gangatope addressed her had a very quietening and soothing effect on her and she replied with great delight, "Yes, it is the good that knows the value of the good ;—is it our Master Gangadhar or is it not ? Come along Master Ganga, let us go." As soon as our Master Ganga heard these flattering remarks from his aunt he was quite mad with joy. Never before had he heard such flattering remarks. He therefore was quite swollen with pride and joy and he thought he was in heaven itself. And the more he began to ponder on those remarks the more did he begin to swell with pride. With

---

In this tale mention has been made of almost all the fishes in their local names. It is very difficult for a translator to find the exact equivalent in English for all the fishes named. The translator has not seen any fish like *Kawoi*, *Goroi*, etc. in England and he therefore does not attempt to render these names into English. Note that the fish which we call *Sole* is not the *Sole* of the British Isles. An aquarium or a pisciculturist may perhaps supply the equivalents, but they will be scientific names and will be of no interest to the lay reader.

every step that he took he swelled more and more and just when he was about to reach the place of meeting he felt so proud that his stomach made a noise as if he had been shot and it burst. The noise that this bursting created seemed like the report of a gun to the members of the assembly, which frightened them to such an extent that each and all of them dispersed in all directions.

The Youngest Child

(*Noomolia Po*)

There were an old couple. In their old age they were blessed with a male child. The father, even after a great deal of thought and worry, was not able to find a suitable name for the child. He therefore hastened one day to an astrologer to help him with a name. The astrologer, after questioning the old man with great minuteness and after taking into consideration that it was a child of his old age and lately born, named him Nomol.

The old man then returned home after presenting the astrologer with a *gamocha* and a small coin for his trouble. Being apprehensive that he might forget it, he went on calling out the name loudly as he was going along. But after a time instead of Nomol (meaning, lately born, youngest of all) he started calling out *Nemel* (do not open or do not let go). On his way home he had to go by the side of a river. A merchant happened to have his boat moored on its bank. Just about the time when the old man was reaching the spot, the merchant had given his men orders to unfasten the moorings As the men were following his orders, the old man passed by shouting *Nemel, Nemel* (do not let got), on heariug which the boatmen approached their master said, "Sir, there goes an old man shouting to us not to unfasten our moorings." The merchant then sent for the old man and asked him why it was that he was asking them not to unfasten the boat The old man however was anxious not to forget the name and thinking that he would forget it if he were to reply to the merchant he went on calling out "Nemel, Nemel" as before. The merchant then lost his temper and angrily muttered that he had waited so long there to start on an auspicious day and

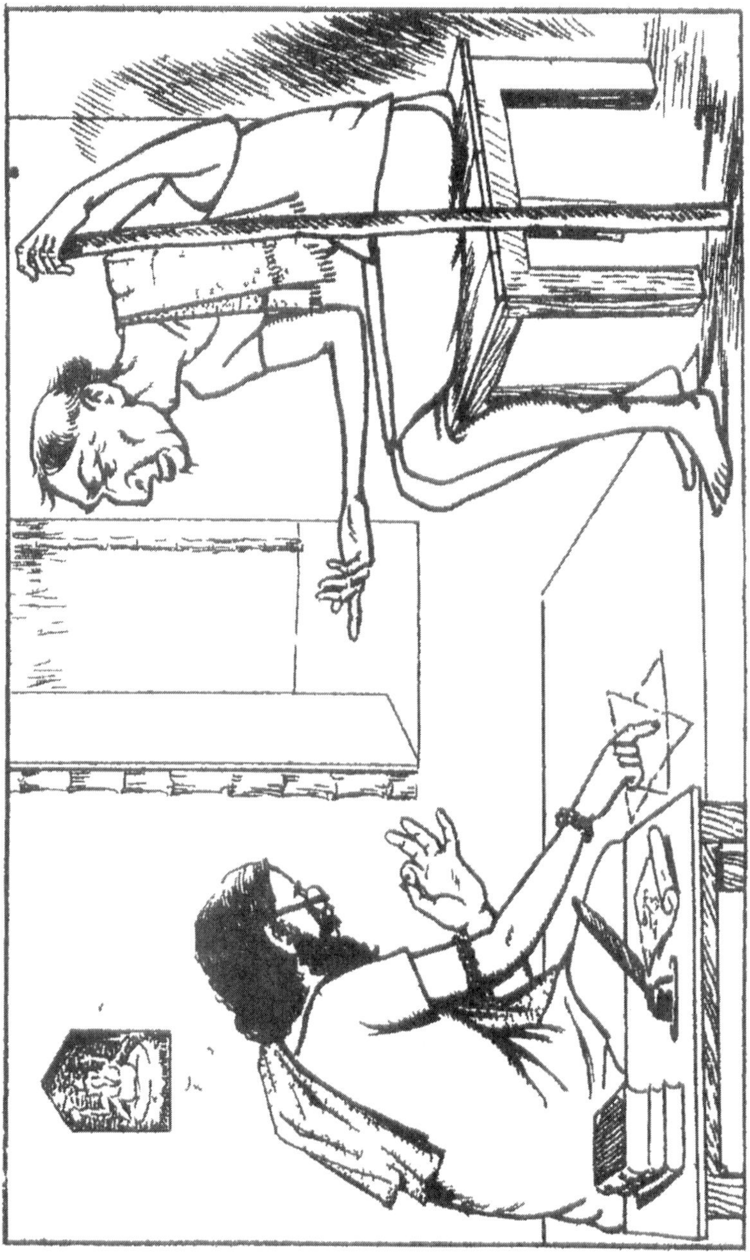

now that he was doing it after consulting the stars and the almanac, this unlucky brute was creating the unnecessary annoyance and obstruction. He then ordered his men to get bold of him and give him a good thrashing. And the men faithfully obeyed him. As he was submitting himself to that operation he forgot what he was saying and started calling out *Nohobor holė* (i.e. has happened what ought not to have happened) He then proceeded homeward shouting out "*Nohobor hole*" when a gaily dressed man passed by him on the way. This fop imagining that he was being ridiculed by the old man because of his ultra-fashionable garb gave him a few good strokes with his cane, After receiving the strokes he forgot what he was saying and began to call out, "This one outdoes the other" and proceeded on his way. A couple of villagers happened to pass him as he was shouting thus and they would have it that he was laughing at their boorish manners. Both of them then fell upon him and knocked him about mercilessly. After all these thrashings he somehow or other managed to crawl home to his wife. He related all that had happened, to his wife and she sympathised with him. She asked him to forget all about it and inquired what name the astrologer had given the child. The old man replied that the beating had taken it all out of him and he had forgotten the name completely.

The old woman like a good wife consoled him and asking him to forget all what had happened advised him to see about ploughing the plot of land attached to their house. She particularly asked him to get tender (using the word Noomolia, the adjective for Nomol) rice plants, and plant them in a particular corner of their garden. On hearing the word "*Noomolia*" mentioned he recalled the name given to his child by the astrologer and turned round saying, "Why on earth did you send me all the way to the astrologer to suffer as I have done if you knew the name yourself ?" He then took revenge on his wife for his recent suffering on the way and smacked, slapped and boxed her to his heart's content.

They then named the child "Nomol" and lived happily ever afterwards.

And we returned home.*

---

* This is another way of finishing up an Assamese tale.

The All-Knowing One

(*Sarabjan*)

There dwelt in a certain village a farmer by the name of *Phoring* (grasshopper). His wife was rather of a selfish disposition The family consisted of the man and his wife—they were without any issue. On rising from bed on a certain rainy morning in the month of Magh (January and February) the farmer told his wife, "Look here, wife, it is a nice and rainy morning I don't feel inclined to take our stereotyped rice to-day. I am just in the mood to have a few cakes. Go and make me some." The wife replied, "Well, where is *Boradhan* (glutinous rice for cakes and pastries) to make the cakes with ? There is not a grain in the house." The husband then was about to give up the idea of indulging in a few cakes that rainy morning—but the wife suggested that he might just as well go and see if any of the neighbours had any ground Boradhan ready for making cakes with and he might ask them to be accommodated with a little. This suggestion made the husband think a while

and having determind upon something, he sallied forth with his Endi (a sort of tough silk much worn as wraps by the people in winter) wrap round him.

Not far from his cottage a neighbour was having his grains trodden out by cattle. Seeing this he sat near the place where it was being done and started a conversation with his neighbour on the weather, crops and the usual topic of the daily meal in vogue among the people. He sat for a long time talking to him—and when all the grains were separated from the chaff, his neighbour removed them away from the straw. When he was thus engaged our friend the farmer complained of an acute pain in his stomach. It was so intense that he writhed with pain and started rolling on the ground and as the grains were scattered he started rolling on them. He recovered after a while and when he returned home he found that there were at least five seers of the grain stuck on to his Endi wrap. It need be hardly said that the pain was shammed with the intention which he carried out so successfully. His wife congratulated him on his successful mission and joyfully started getting the rice ready for the cakes. She sunned and dried them and made them into powder. After she had seen to her husband's meal in the evening she started baking the cakes. Phoring feeling very sleepy after his meal retired to bed. The wife after baking 12 *buri* (score) cakes arranged them on a platter of cane. She then satisfied her hunger with most of them herself leaving just a few for her husband on a plate covered over for the next morning. When she went to bed she woke her husband up and said, "I have finished baking the cakes, but let us come to an understanding—whoever of us will wake and leave the bed first to-morrow morning will get one third of the cakes and the other will get the rest." Phoring as a good docile husband agreed to her proposal.

Next morning neither of them would leave the bed. The Sun was up and it was getting near noon—yet would they not stir. They pretended to snore and sleep on. The husband being mindful of his duties of looking after his fields at last made up his mind to forego the pleasure of having two-thirds of the cake and rose When the wife saw this she said to him that as he had got up first he would get one-third only. The husband said, "Alright, you are welcome to the two-thirds." But when he went to eat the cakes he found to his great surprise that there were but a few on the plate and on inquiring from his wife where the rest of the cakes were, she replied, "How could there be more ? All that I baked are on the plate there. You had better take your share and leave me the rest." The husband was astonished—'Could there be,' he thought 'only these few cakes of the five seers of rice ? Impossible.' Then his eyes happened to light on the cane platter hung on the wall and there were just the tell-tale marks of as many cakes as were baked. He counted the marks and saying nothing to his wife had his share of the cakes without a word Then when his wife came to give him his usual morning betel, taking it in his hand he made up a cryptic rhyme for the occasion and gave her to understand that he knew all about her doings of the night before, When he mentioned the actual number of cakes she was quite flabbergasted.

She was very much ashamed of herself on being found out like this. When she went to fetch water from the river, woman-like, she told the other women who were there that her husband was a marvel and could divine other peoples' thoughts and know what they did. The whole village then was apprised of this fact and he got the sobriquet of *Sarabjan* or All-knowing attached to his name in less than no time. And his fame reached far and wide.

Just about this time a villager happened to miss his black cow. After searching for her for five long days fruitlessly, on learning of the great gifts of Phoring he approached him and begged of him to find out where his cow was. As luck would have it Phoring had seen the animal grazing just that very morning in the thatch field behind his house. He therefore without any hesitation directed him to look for her behind his house. The man accordingly went as directed and was awarded by the sight of his cow. After this it spread far and wide that Phoring was really a *Sarabjan* and there was ample proof of it This news in course of time reached the king.

At about this time a gold necklace worth a lac of rupees was missing in the palace, and when the king came to know of Phoring's power he sent for him after every effort to find it out had proved unsuccessful. When the king's officers informed him of the king's command he was thunderstruck. What was he to do? If he did not obey he would be killed, the same fate would overtake him if could not find the lost article, and it would mean the same thing if he were to give the truth out and say that he was not really a *Sarabjan*.

He was completely at a loss as to what he was to do. Leaving it to fate and after praying to God he approached the king. When he was informed of the *Sarabjan's* arrival the king received him cordially and with out-stretched arms invited him to take a seat near the throne He was then taken to the inner apartments and was entertained with dainties, one of the items being curdled milk.

Now the king had two queens Their names were Madoi and Hadoi. It was Hadoi the junior queen who had stolen the necklace And when she knew that the *Sarabjan* was requisitioned for the purpose she was all in a flutter She peeped through an aperture in the wall to see what the man was like. Phoring himself however was also quaking with fear and as he saw the plate of curdled millk or *doi* befoie him he muttered aloud, "Ha-doi (meaning, Alas, Doi ! It was the name of the queen also), let me taste of you to-day, no one knows how the king will decide to-morrow."

The queen Hadoi heard this and she thought the *Sarabjan* was referring to her. She began to say to herself, "I am done for now, the *Sarabjan* has found me out." And she then came out, casting aside her modesty, and said to him,

"*Sarabjan*, pray do not give me away. I can assure you I will make it worth your while for you." *Sarabjan* then had no difficulty in finding out how the matter stood and he at once discovered that the thief was no other than the queen Hadoi herself. He, assuming his most serious demeanour said, "Your Majesty may rest assured that I shall not divulge your Majesty's secret—but my advice to you is that the necklace should forthwith be replaced in His Majesty's cash box as it was before." She did as she was told.

The next day when the king held his court he requested the *Sarabjan* to tell the assembly who it was that had stolen the necklace. In reply, making his obeisance, he said, "Your Majesty's humble subject as I am, my calculations do not tell me that your necklace is stolen at all. I find that it is still in Your Majesty's cash-box." The cash-box was sent for immediately and it was found that the *Sarabjan* was quite correct ; the necklace was in its usual place. This was indeed too much for the public, and their faith in him was more than confirmed. The king awarded him free grants of land and other estates and found for him an office in his Majesty's household.

One day the king just to test the *Sarabjan's* knowledge held a grasshopper in his grasp and asked him what it was that he had in his hand. He was at his wit's end and as was his wont he muttered aloud to himself in rhyme to this effect. "Once I counted up and was right and on one occasion I saw it with my own eyes and was correct ; the necklace made its appearance when I but called out Hadoi ; but now I find that poor *Phoring's* (grasshopper, his own name) end is near."

The king was not aware of his name ; he just knew him as the *Sarabjan.* When, therefore, he heard "the poor grasshopper's end is near," he thought that the man was alluding to the grass-hopper in his grasp. He let the grasshopper off and as a reward for his marvellous powers he then and there presented Phoring with the gorgeous suit of clothes he was then wearing.

Our cloths had to be sent to the wash and we returned home.

The Tale Of A Singara Fish

(Eta Singara Machor Kotha)

One day a poor man went to fish in the river. He fished the whole day and his labours were awarded with but one solitary Singara-fish He took it home and was about to get it ready for the oven when the Singara called aloud, "Brother, I am the king of the Singaras—pray don't you eat me, I shall always look after your cow." When he heard the fish say these words he did not eat it After giving it a good meal the next day he sent it to graze his cow in the field. The Singara climbed up the cow and sitting on the top-end of her tail drove her about in the neighbouring fields. This continued for a long time. One day as the Singara was grazing her about in the fields it happened to take her towards the forest. Now there lived in that forest a monster who, when he saw the cow, advanced open-mouthed with great glee. The Singara in a commanding tone said to the monster, "Hold on, hold on, don't be in a hurry ; if you can fight me and manage to quell me it is then that you will be able to eat my cow, otherwise beware there will be an end of all your pranks." The monster was greatly amused with the boasting of the tiny little Singara and when he went to crush with his fingers it pricked him with his thorny fin so hard and at the same time clutched him so tight that the monster was only too glad to get out of its clutch ; he said, "Let me go, please, I will give you whatever you like. Please let me go." The Singara raplied, "If you wish me to let you off, first tell me what you wiil give me." The monster then vomited out a ring and said, "Take this ring and keep it carefully folded in a banana leaf and look after it well, for you will find that it has such great virtues that it will transform your house into a house of gold and you will be laden with silver and gold." The Singara then refrained from pricking him and taking the ring he drove the cow towards their home. On reaching home he gave the ring to his master and when the master followed the instructions carefully it all came to be true and his house was transformed into a house of gold and he was laden with plenty of silver and gold He was so happy that he then and there gave his daughter in marriage with the Singara. They lived there happily for some time. The Singara, as it was afterwards found out, was a

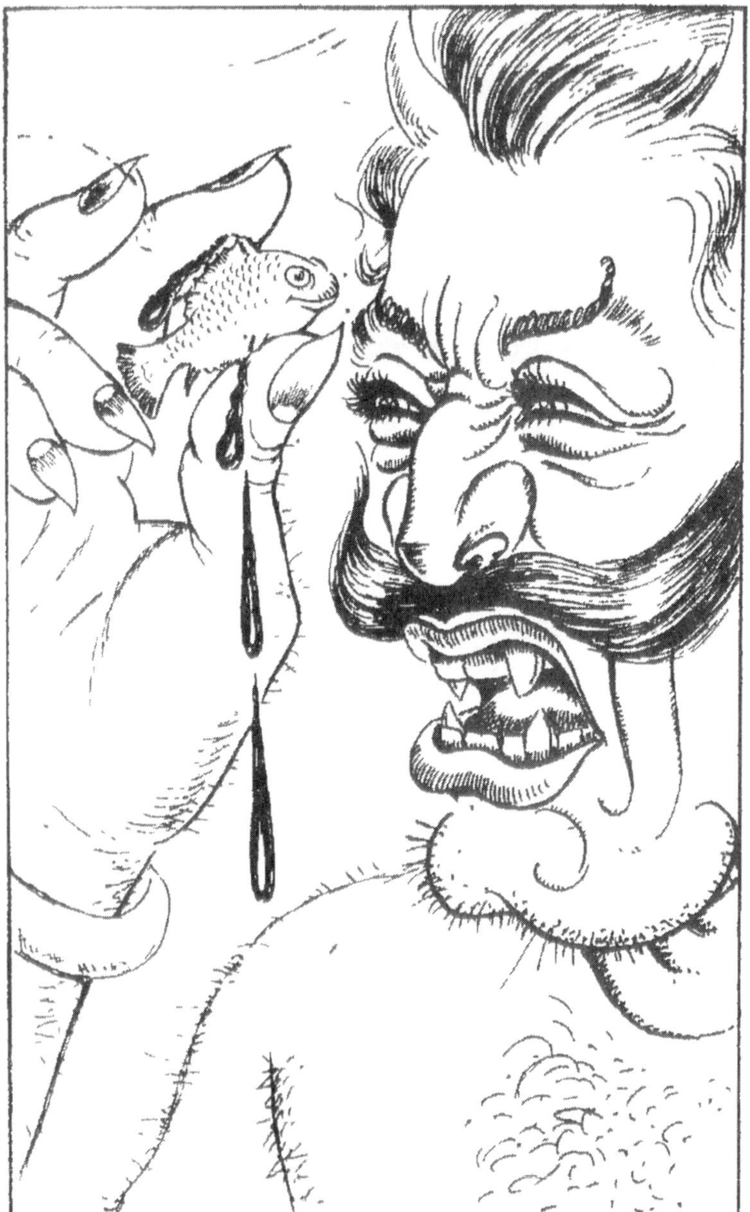

man in disguise. One day as the Singara was bathing in the river leaving his fish body on the bank, the wife came and burnt it. Then the Singara could no longer remain as a fish ; he was obliged to retain his human form. He then throve and became a prosperous and a portly person. They all lived happily ever after.

* The owl is on the roof,
And my tale, all false it is,
The areca-nut has opened out its calyx,
Who will go where ?

---

* This is also another meaningless but amusing way of finishing up a tale.

The Tale Of A Strong Man

(*Eta Bolee Manuh*)

Once upon a time in a certain good king's dominion there were a very big elephant and a tiger. Both these two together made it simply uncomfortable for his subjects to continue to live in his dominion. The king's attempts to get rid of these two unruly subjects were fruitless and when he found that all his efforts were of no avail, he proclaimed it by beat of drum that any one who would kill them would be amply rewarded. This naturally tempted a great many people, but unfortunately no one could get at them.

It so happened that a poor, unfortunate dejected creature, tired and weary of this life, prior to commiting suicide was wending his way towards that kiug's dominion with some poison mixed with food—his ground rice. He felt thirsty on his way and leaving his bundle under a tree went to get a drop of water from a river hard by. Just then the unruly elephant appeared on the spot aud ate all the ground rice up. The poison that was mixed with the food worked like magic and the elephant died almost immediately after. When the king was informed of the elephant's death he naturally was mightily pleased and was curious to know how he came by his death. The man who was found near the place of occurrence was produced before the king. He was questioned by his Majesty and he informed him that he killed the animal with one blow of his hand.

The king was highly pleased with him and gave him a great deal of money as a reward for removing the elephant from his dominion for good. He then informed the man that there was a tiger in his kingdom who created havoc in the neighbourhood and if this animal were removed by anybody he would be highly awarded by the state. The man undertook to kill that animal also. The king commanded that the tiger must be killed the day after next. He came forward like a man good and true and agreed to kill the tiger within the appointed time. He then devised various plans of killing the tiger.

On the appointed day he entered the forest with several coils of rope and a huge bamboo with much misgiving and trepidation of heart.

He climbed a very big tree in the forest and started making as much noise as he was capable of, which disturbed all the birds. Naturally they too made a great deal of noise. The tiger approaching the tree asked the man on it, "Brother, what is it that you are teaching the birds ?" He replied that he was teaching them music. The tiger then begged of him to teach him too. The man thereupon replied, "Well, friend, you know you are a tiger and I am only a human being, what is the guarantee that you will not eat me ?" The tiger in reply said that he would bind himself down not to molest him in any way and took three oaths for the purpose. The man climbed down the tree and tying the tiger's feet with the cords as securely as possible began belabouring him with the bamboo. Not being able to stand the beating any longer he said, "Brother, let me go, I don't wish to learn any more, I have had enough of learning." The man replied, "No, no, you have not had enough. You must learn thoroughly and well " He continued to beat the tiger in consequence whereof he died.

The man brought the tiger to the king in great triumph. The king was quite pleased with this brave man and he said, "I will get a strong man to fight with you—if you can beat that man

I will give you much more than what I have already done." He then sent for the other strong man and they slept the night together before the great event was coming off. The man addressing the strong man said, "Brother, I have killed both a tiger as well as an elephant with one good blow of this hand. How will you stand against me? I feel sorry for you, friend. It would not do for you to kick the bucket so soon, would it? In your prime of life too." The strong man hearing this quaked with fear and made good his escape that very night The next morning the king had all the neighbourhood scoured to look for his strong man and not being successful in finding him amply rewarded the man who rid the kingdom of the tiger and the elephant. Peace then reigned all over his kingdom.

The jack tree bore fruit and I then returned.*

---

* This too is a form of ending a tale.

The Tale Of The Kite's Daughter

Chilanee Jiyekor Sadhu

Once upon a time there was a potter in a certain village. He was wealthy but sonless. His wife bore him daughters only. This was a constant source of worry to him. After a time his wife became pıegnant and the potter addressing his wife said,—"If you are delivered of a daughter this time—better look out—as sure as I am your husband, I will sell you to the Nagas."

Just as her time was approaching the potter's wife went to her mother's house. But how unfortunate she was—she was delivered of a daughter this time too ! This made her tremble with fear and before the husband could ever come to hear of it she wrapped the child up wrth some cloth round it and placing it in an earthen pot covered it over with another. She then threw it into the river. The little thing in the earthen pot drifted down the river. A washerman seeing the earthen pot thus drifting along in mid-stream became curious to know what it contained. He swam to it and on uncovering the lid found to his utter dismay that it contained a new-born babe. Just as he was making for the bank with a view to taking the child to his wife, a kite pounced upon it and flew with it to her nest on an banyan tree. The kite was simply enamoured of the child. Her childish beauty capivated her and she made up her mind to rear the baby herself She made her as comfortable in her nest as she could. Whenever the kite saw anything good and thought it would be good for the child she would pounce upon it and would feed the baby with it. She brought the child up with great care and the child grew into a lovely little girl. If she happened to see any fine dresses about left for drying in the sun she would pick them up and bring them to her child. One day the royal princess was bathing in the river leaving her clothes and jewellery on the bank. The kite happening to see them pounced upon them and made away with them to her child. The kite thus furnished her with brushes, combs, mirrors, vermilion pots, oil cups and in short whatever else she could seize upon.

As time wore on, the little girl grew into a charming young woman. She however knew no home but her tree. One day the kite said to

her, "My child, you have now grown into a lovely woman and I cannot be at ease leaving you here all alone. I have to make very long journeys sometimes. And so let me tell you what you are to do. If you are in danger when I am away and want me badly, you will only have to sing :—

> O the breeze that shakes the leaves
> Of this banyan tree,
> Bring my mother kite
> At once before me.

I will come and appear before you wherevcr I may be.

One very warm day the girl was combing her hair when a merchant feeling tired on account of the extreme heat rested a while under the tree. There was not a single soul anywhere near it. A hair dropped just on the very lap of the merchant. He was at a loss to find how there could be a human hair in that solitary place. And it was very long too—seven cubits in length. He looked about for a long time but could see nobody there. Happening to look up he saw a very beautiful girl combing her hair very comfortably on a branch of that tree. The merchant astonished to find such a beautiful girl in such a place under such circumstances addressing himself to her said, "Who are you? Are you a human being or a goddess? An angel or an evil spirit? What are you? Tell me why you are on the top of a tree, and at this time of the day too." The poor girl had never seen a man before —this was her first sight of a man. She was so frightened that she did not know what answer to make and she sang out as she was taught by her foster mother the kite She sang :—

O the breeze that shakes the leaves
Of this banyan tree,
Bring my mother kite
At once before me."

And the kite appeared on the scene immediately. She asked, "Child, why do you call me?" In reply her daughter pointed with her finger to the man under the tree As soon as the kite set her eyes on the handsome and young merchant she thought to herself that if the man was as good as he looked it would be an excellent idea to get him for her daughter's husband. She came down and sitting beside the merchant related the whole history of the girl. The merchant said, "I am blessed with the goods of this world. I am well off. I have at present seven wives. If that is no objection, I shall be very happy to make her my wife and I can assure you I shall look after her comfort and well-being to the best of my ability. She will never have a day's trouble or worry; and she will never be in want." The kite was pleased with the straightforward and honourable way of address the merchant had. After a few moment's deliberation she agreed to his proposal. She however had some difficulty in persuading her daughter to leave her and go in company with the merchant. She brought her down and gave her in marriage with the merchant. The kite then begged of him with tears in her eyes to look after her dear daughter and she whispered in her ears that whenever she wanted her, her daughter had only to sing out as she had been taught and she would appear on the scene

The merchant then took his young bride home. He loved her and had all her wants attended to. His other seven wives however were extremely jealous of her good looks and they thought that now that their husband had a young and beautiful wife he would soon forget them and their husband would love them no longer. All the seven wives then tried their best to give her a bad time of it.

One day they all came to her and said, "It seems you think yourself to be quite a cut above us—we have to cook and do all the household work every day and you do nothing but eat and sleep. Go and cook for us to-day," She never knew what it was to cook—she had never cooked before. Not finding any way out of the difficulty she began weeping bitterly. She then went to the orchard behind the house and sang out for her mother as she had been taught to. The kite, true to her word, appeared before her and asked her, "What is the matter? Why do you call me?" She then told her all about her trouble. When she finished, the kite said, "Is that all? Don't worry, my dear, I will show you the way how to cook. Fill a cooking pot with water and throw a grain of rice into it; in another pot just in the same way throw a little vegetable in. And then place one lighted firewood under each pot: You will have to do nothing after it—leave the kitchen then and sit outside. You will find that you have an inexhaustible quantity of rice and vegetables to feed as many people as you wish to." The kite then flew away and her daughter following her instructions was rewarded with the most satisfactory result. When they sat down to their meal they dug holes under their plates and as soon as the kite's daughter would serve them with food, instead of eating they would throw it into the holes and they would ask for more. It was an inexhaustible store and at last the co-wives had to give in.

One day they asked her to sweep the cowshed. As soon as she entered the cowshed she sang out for her mother. (The only difference in the couplet being, that instead of the banyan tree she used the banana tree because that was plentiful in the orchard). When the kite came she told her what her co-wives had asked her to do. She replied, "Oh, that is nothing—take one stick from the broom and rub it gently along the length of the cowshed. You will find that the whole shed will be swept clean." The girl did as she was told by her mother—and the cowshed was swept so clean as it never had been swept before. It looked quite bright. The merchant was very pleased with her and loved her more and more day after day.

The Chait Bihu was approaching. The merchant gave five seers of cotton to each of his eight wives and asked them to make him clothes for the festival, adding that he would like to see who made the best. The seven wives set to work at once; they drew the fibres, separated them from the seed, span the cotton and started weaving in less than no time; but the merchant's eighth wife, not knowing how to do all these sat depressed and dejected. Her co-wives said to each other, "It is all up with her, she is cornered now. She does not know anything about spinning and weaving—let us see how she does her husband's clothes." She then cried for her mother in the usual way from the orchard and as usual the kite appeared on the spot immediately She asked. "What is it, dear ? Why do you call me again ?" Her daughter totd her how the co-wives were weaving and she did not know how to do it. The kite replied, "Don't you worry, my dear, you will be able to make your husband's clothes. First thing you do after I have left you will be to get four bamboo caskets and then fill them up with some cotton ; after you have done that plug them up. Don't do anything else. When your husband will ask for his clothes on the Bihu day you will just hand him the caskets and he will get his clothes ready." Saying this she left her daughter. The girl did as she was told. Her co-wives with a great deal of show and pomp went on weaving and when they saw that instead of doing her work she was doing nothing, they were all mad with joy and said to each other, "We are in for some fun now, our co-wife does not know how to spin or weave and when our husband will ask for his clothes from her she won't be able to give him anything. And won't there be some fun when the merchant will go for her ?"

On the great day all his seven wives gave the merchant seven suits of clothes (Coat, Dhoti, Chaddar, and Gamocha), the eighth wife gave him only four caskets. The co-wives when they saw her presenting her husband only four caskets, laughed in great glee and the merchant too was very angry. He asked her, "What are all these ? Where are my clothes ?" She replied, "You just open them and see." When the merchant opened them there appeared from each one of them fine wearing apparels. These clothes were so fine that the others in comparison with these looked like coarse rags. The merchant therefore tore into pieces the clothes given by his seven elder wives and accepted and wore the clothes given by his eighth.

Gradually it came to the knowledge of the seven wives that their co-wife used to be instructed on all these matters by a kite. They put their heads together and tried to devise a plan of doing away with her. One of them found out somehow how the kite used to be called by her. This co-wife imitating the girl's voice called her to the cowshed. The kite ignorant of this conspiracy to do away with her came there As soon as she entered, the jealous co-wife gave her several good cuts with the broom. She was then buried under a heap of cow-dung. Her daughter did not even have an inkling of this matter. She sang out many a time for the kite but how could she come to her? When the kite would not come to her even after she sang out for her several times she came to the conclusion that her co-wives must have killed her When this dawned upon her she sobbed bitterly for her foster-mother who loved her so much.

Sometime after this the merchant happened to leave home on businesss and at the time of his departure he particularly ordered his seven wives that they must look after his youngest wife with care.

A few weeks after the merchant's departure a tradesman came to the village and moored his boat very near the merchant's house. He had with him for sale such articles as combs, mirrors and looking-glasses, vermilion, scented oil and other things that please womenfolk the most. The merchant's wives thought this to be an excellent opportunity of doing away with their eye-sore the youngest co-wife. They went to the tradesman and bought various articles from him and as their value they said they would give one of the most beautiful girls he ever set his eyes on. They described her good looks in such a way that the tradesman was anxious to have her in exchange of the articles They went in a very friendly way to their co-wife and they told her what lovely things the tradesman had brought; —they were going there, would she come? She replied, "Sisters, I do not want anything, if you like you may go. And besides, he (husband)[*] has specially asked me not to go anywhere." They were not going to give it up in a hurry, they coaxed her and cajoled her and at last she had to give in. They all went together to the riverside and made her get into the boat as if to see the tradesman's wares better. When she got in they made a signal as previously arranged, whereat the boatmen cut the moorings and the tradesman disappeared with the girl.

The tradesman on reaching home made the merchant's wife look after his dried fish. His house was just on the river and the unfortunate

---

* Indian wives never call their husbands by their —as a rule, "he" is husband when a wife uses this pronoun.

girl used to look after the fish on the river bank exposed to the heat of the sun. She would in her sadness sing a song of her own composition to this effect,—

My mother was a potter's wife who let
me drift along the river ;
My mother kite brought me up.
A merchant prince did marry me ;
My seven co-wives did sell me to a fisherman,
And the fisherman now has made me the
custodian of his dried fish.

One day as the merchant's wife was singing this way the merchant happened to pass by the river. He heard her sing and recognising her voice, ordered his men to stop the boat. He went near her and asked her the cause of her wailing. When he heard all, he made himself known to her and giving her new clothes to wear took her home He put her in a box with a small hole through which to breathe in. When he reached home he had this box removed to his bed-room along with his other boxes. On seeing all his seven wives there he inquired of his eighth wife from them. They all replied that she had gone to her mother's house long ago and had not returned. The merchant said, "Well, I am afraid you have done something to her. I shall see however whether you are speaking the truth or not. I am going to put you to test in a minute." He ordered his men to dig a very deep and wide pit and had it filled with thorny branches and twigs. He then had a thread fixed between its two sides, traversing the whole pit. He ordered his wives to go across the pit crawling over the thread. "If", he said, "you are really innocent, nothing will happen to you, if on the other hand you are guilty, you will be killed." They all attempted to go across as they were commanded by their husband. Six of them failed in the attempt and they fell into the thorny pit and the seventh wife succeeded in going across. She was declared to be not guilty by her husband ; and she really was so, as when her co-wives were busy in luring the innocent Kite's daughter into the tradesman's boat she was busy cooking and she knew nothing of the underhand transaction. The thread did not give way even though she crawled seven times over it.

The merchant then had his six wives buried alive in that same pit. He then lived happily ever afterwards with his seventh wife and the kite's daughter.

Our clothes had to be sent to the wash and we returned.

Toola And Teja

(Toola Aru Teja)

Once upon a time a well-to-do farmer had two wives—the younger one was his favourite and the elder was not. He had by his elder wife a son named Kanai and a daughter named Teja. The favourite had but one—a daughter, and her name was Toola. She was a little older than Teja. His favourite wife used to make Teja and Kanai's lives miserable by putting them to all sorts of tortures and sufferings. The unfortunate, hen-pecked husband could not show any indications of fatherly love and affection towards them for fear of his wife. They were not allowed a single good meal or even any decent clothes and they had to turn out early in the morning to graze the cows in the field after breakfasting on some cold stale rice of the previous night. On the other hand Toola had the best of every thing to eat and to wear. When the farmer would return after his morning work his favourite wife would have ready for him hot rice and curry and numerous other hot viands of various sorts—but he, after his long morning's work, far rather preferred to have cold rice and boiled fish in his elder wife's broken hut to the hot dishes. And when the younger wife found that the farmer frequented her co-wife's hut for his meals she started contriving some plan how she could do away with her.

One day the younger wife invited her co-wife to fish with a jokai. (It is a conical basket with a handle—a fishing implement much in vogue among women and children. They go knee-deep and sometimes waist-deep with the basket which they dip into the water for fishing.) The elder wife's jokai was full of nice big fishes at the first dip and the younger one had hers full of crabs and other fishes. This enraged the favourite to such an extent that she lost all control over herself. After they had finished their morning sport the junior wife suggested that they should have a dip in the big pond hard by. Prior to bathing she requested her co-wife to give her a good scrubbing and scouring as she was full of mud and dirt and she also in her turn would give the other one a good scrubbing. The elder wife gladly assented to this proposal and she scrubbed and scoured her co-wife gladly ; and when the junior wife in her turn started scrubbing her co-wife's person she gave her a push into the pond saying with some muttered incantation, "Go and be a big tortoise." After she had done that she trod on the jokai and breaking it into bits threw it into a jungle hard by. When she returned home alone her co-wife's children were anxious in not seeing their mother. They approached her in fear and screwing their courage up asked her gently, "Auntie, have you seen our mother—do you know where she has gone?" The step-mother snapped up saying, "How do I know where your mother has gone? Does she ever ask me as to where she is to go?" The husband too for fear of his younger wife was afraid to inquire after his other wife—he concluded that she must have met with her death somehow or other and never alluded to her again. The poor little orphans looked high and low for their mother but not being successful in their search sobbed silently and bitterly. As usual they had to turn out early for their morning work for they well knew that if they did not do so they would be punished by their step-mother.

One day as they were grazing their cows in the heat of the mid-day sun they felt very thirsty and went to the big pond for a drink of water. There was stillness all round and there was nobody else about near the spot. The tortoise called out to them saying, "My dear Teja and Kanai, your step-mother pushed me here and has by her wicked incantations turned me into a tortoise. You look very tired, dears, it does not seem as if you had anything to eat for days. Go and pluck two arum leaves. I shall give you some sweet rice which I have brought from the water-

god and eat it in there. Don't you however tell anybody about me. If your stepmother were to hear of me she would put me to death," And after they had finished their sweet rice their mother asked them to come there and eat some of it every day. They used to go to the pond daily and eat sweet rice. Now the step-mother was surprised to find that though she did not give them much to eat Teja and Kanai looked better and better every day whereas her Toola who was given the best of every thing, instead of looking better looked thinner and thinner. She concluded that they must eat somewhere as they went out grazing the cattle. The next morning as they were going out she asked her Toola to accompany them asking her to keep a look out to see if Teja and Kanai had anything to eat anywhere. Teja, Kanai and their mother were in a fix that day as it was not their intention to let Toola see what they did. It so happened that a cow had strayed from the flock and Teja asked her sister to drive it back. When Toola was away they hurriedly ate the sweet rice and when they were throwing the arum leaves away she returned and saw them in the act. Toola begged and entreated to be told what they had eaten but they would not. At last her pitiful entreaties melted their hearts and they said, "Well, there is nothing more to be given you. If you like, go and lick off the remnants from the leaves, but don't you tell your mother anything about it. If you do, you will never get such a nice thing to eat again." Toola then picked up the leaves and licked the remnants off. When they returned home the mother was surprised to find her daughter so refreshed that she looked like a ripe orange. Suspecting that her daughter too must have had a share of their food she began to question her. The daughter would not tell her. She however had to give it up and tell everything when her mother threatened to rub raw chillies on her eyes. The mother then came to the conclusion that it was their mother the tortoise who gave them always to eat. She started contriving some plan to do away with it One day therefore she had some potsherds brought and had them placed under her bed. She then took to her bed and when the husband came to enquire what had happened to her, instead of replying to his questions she began to turn in her bed from one side to another, thus breaking the potsherds She then told her husband that all her bones were breaking and that unless something was done quickly she would die. Being very anxious for her health he sent for the old woman of the village who could calculate and asked her what was the best thing to be done in the circumstances. This old woman was already in her pay and she had taught her to say that on being asked by her husband what would be the remedy for her she was to say that the flesh of the tortoise in the big pond would cure her malady at once. As soon as the husband was told that the tortoise flesh would cure her he begged of the whole village to go and fish it out. All the villagers, men, women, children turned out in a body to help the well-to-do farmer. As soon as however Teja and Kanai came to know of it they ran for all they were worth to inform their mother of the impending calamity. Their mother asked them not to worry and she said, "I am not going to be caught in anybody's net , after all attempts when they would give up, you would come with a broken jokai into the pond and I would come up in it at the first dip. Don't you however partake of my flesh When the cook will get me ready for the kitchen you had better ask him to let you have my two fore-paws and bury them by the pond here I shall grow into a China-rose plant and it will be of great use to you in your time of need "

All the villagers turned out to a man to catch the tortoise They however simply helped to make the water more muddy though they had all manners of fishing implements with them When they all gave it up as something impossible to do, the two little children walked into the water and expressed their desire to catch the tortoise. When the villagers heard it they all broke into a loud guffaw saying, "The young uns will catch it, will they ? Well, let them have a try, that is all." Teja then dipped the jokai into the water and lo and behold ! There came the tortoise up It took their breath away.

As soon as the favourite wife heard that the tortoise was caught she began to feel better at once. As taught beforehand they asked for the two fore-paws from the cook and they buried them by the pond. Every one of the household made a good meal of the tortoise flesh that day except Teja and Kanai who had their usual starvation fare.

There grew on the spot where the two fore-paws were buried a shaddock tree and a China-rose plant (hibiscus) They brightened the whole neighbourhood, one by its fruits and the other by its flowers and every day the two little orphans would come and sit under the shade of these two plants and talk with their mother.

One of the princes of the country happened to pass that way with a cortege of a retinue of elephants, horses aud sedan-chairs. The prince felt tempted to taste one of the lovely fruits and sent his secretary to go and pluck him a few.

Teja and Kanai were there at the time and as soon as they saw what the prince's secretary was going to do they called out, "These plants are ours and we won't let you pluck any fruit or flower unless the prince comes and asks for them himself." When the secretary informed the prince of their demands he good-naturedly descended form his sedan-chair and approached the children. As soon as the prince approached them Kanai kneeling before the prince addressed him thus, "If your Highness would wed my sister we would most gladly let you have some fruits and flowers, otherwise not." The prince was charmed with the lovely appearance of the girl and said, "Your request is granted. I shall most gladly wed your sister but she is young yet. I promise to do so however as soon as she grows a little older." Teja had a pet myna whom she used to carry about with her, feeding it with worms and insects while grazing the cows and Kanai had a pomegranate plant which he used to carry about with him. Placing them both at the feet of the prince Kanai said, "Your Highness, we are poor, and perhaps your Highness may forget us ; therefore I beg leave to present you with this myna and this little plant, and when the bird will begin to talk and this plant will bear fruit your Highness will know that Teja is grown up sufficiently for you to wed her, and will come and take her to your territory "

The prince agreed to this reasonable request and returned to his dominions with the myna, the plant and the fruits and flowers. It need hardly be said that Kanai was taught by his mother to say all he had said When he reached his destination the prince had the pomegranate plant planted near his bedroom windows and the myna's cage was hung in the verandah near by.

Then as time and tide would wait for no man the pomegranate plant grew, it blossomed, and gradually the blossom became a fruit and ripened into a delicious pomegranate. The myna too started chirping and talking. But the prince was entirely oblivious of Teja.

One day just as the prince was enjoying his siesta the myna sang out in rhyme, as all good mynas of folktale celebrity do, and reminded him of the fact that poor Teja, far far away had grown into a woman He looked about him to find out who it was that had sung, but not seeing anyone he continued his siesta

But the myna would not give up—he sang out again after some time to the same effect. It proved successful on this occasion however and

Teja was brought back to the prince's memory at once on hearing the myna's words.

He saw that the pomegranate plant had borne fruit. The prince then ordered his retinue to be ready and started on his way to wed Teja. He kept his princess entirely in the dark however as to where he was going. The princess being curious asked one of her old maid-servants as to where he was going. The old servant was equal to the occasion and gave her the undesirable news that the prince was going to get a co-wife for her —a daughter of a prosperous farmer living not very far from there The princess on hearing this cried as loudly as she was capable of crying but her old nurse consoled her by saying, "Don't cry my sweet, but do as I tell you. When the prince will bring the girl to-morrow—be ready at the landing stage, and forbid her to land, do so by following her to every possible landing stage But if however by any chance she does land notwithstanding your protests, do this —Place two banana plants by the gate as a symbol of welcome but instead of fixing them firmly on to the ground fix them gently so that they would be knocked off by the touch of her dress as she would enter. Take off the hinges from the door so that when she would go to close it, it would tumble down ;

break the leg of the chair on which she is likely to sit and place it in such a way as it would not be possible to detect that it was broken but no sooner will she sit upon it, it would give way. Do the same with the bedstead so that the bed will break as soon as they would retire for the night. All this will convince the prince that she is a woman of ill omen and he is then sure to banish her." The princess promised to follow her nurse's instructions faithfully.

The prince reached Teja's village and wedded her. As she was leaving her father's roof with her husband she asked him for a portion of her mother's furniture, crockery, jewellery and other articles.* Her step-mother as soon as she heard it snapped up by saying that she won't part with even as much as a straw. Teja was quite upset at this behaviour and without taking leave of anybody else she left with her husband. She only said,—

"My one and only brother
Must come with me for ever."

And without looking back for once she left her father's home and as she did so all her father's belongings followed her. The father was thunder-

*Teja sang out her request but for my inability to do justice to the song I have refrained from translating it.

struck, thinking that he was going to be denuded of all his property and he begged and entreated of her to look back even for once. Her father's pleadings made her turn her head back ever so slightly which resulted in her father's having a quarter of his belongings left to him and the remaining three-fourths followed her. Even now therefore when a daughter leaves her father's roof with her husband she always turns back and if she forgets to do that all her father's belongings go with her.

True to the directions she had received from her maid the princess was awaiting at the landing stage for the arrival of the prince with his newly wedded wife. As soon as the boat reached the bank, the princess said,

"Land not, land not, O thou witch Teja,
This be the prince's bathing ghat."

Teja then attempted to land in another place, the princess did the same thing, saying that that was the prince's kitchen *ghat*. She followed Teja about from place to place forbidding to land her at every stage.

Teja complained to her husband that she was not allowed to land by her elder co-wife and she was being called a witch by her. The prince as a good husband consoled her by saying that Teja would occupy the throne with him and he landed with her at his bathing ghat.

As soon as she entered the palace the two banana plants which were fixed by the gate fell down as she walked in. The prince's elder wife banteringly sang at her :—

"Oh, you witch Teja, whereform do
you come,
You who tumble the plants as you
come home."

At which Teja looking to the prince for protection, sang :—

"Listen, my husband, good
king and rich,
Elder sister mine doth call me a witch"

The prince then consoled her as before by saying that she would share his throne with him and she need not mind what his other wife said.

The door hinges came off and the door tumbled down The princes taunted and chid her in the same way—Teja complained to her husband and the prince consoled her the same way. The bedstead gave way and the same thing was repeated again.

Be that as it may the prince and Teja lived happily as husband and wife. And Teja's stepmother was bursting with envy and anger at such blissful happiness as her step-daughter was enjoying. She was dying with envy because the prince did not wed her Toola. She therefore thought out a plan and making a great pretence of love for Teja paid a visit to her son-in-law's house. No sooner she saw Teja than she embraced and kissed her saying, "Oh, the sweet little pet, she must be longing to get home for a few days after so long an absence! Her father seems to be buried in his farm work and does not bestow a single moment's thought on his poor darling—but I am after all a mother and cannot keep her away any longer—will you let her off for a few days, son?" The prince could not very well avoid such a kind invitation for Teja and he allowed her to go. Before her step-mother had come Teja had started weaving a fine cloth in her loom and she had to leave it to her chagrin unfinished, to go with her step-mother.

Though Teja was to all intents and purposes receiving the kindest of care and attention there the step-mother was all along on the alert to find some means of doing her an evil turn. And it was not long in coming.

One day Toola said to her, "Will you let me wear just for once, my dear little sister, the jewellery which the prince has given you?" Teja did not see through this and said, "Certainly, by all means, dear, do wear them." She then took off all the jewellery from her person and put them on Toola. Just at this moment the step-mother suggested that she would do Teja's hair for her—it need not be said that Toola had expressed the desire of wearing her sister's jewellery at the suggestion of her mother. Unsuspecting Teja sat down to let her step-mother do her hair.

After a little while her step-mother knocked her head with an iron pin muttering an incantation and adding the words, "Be a *salika* (myna)". Teja was no longer a human being and she became a bird

When the prince sent his messengers for the princess the next day—her mother dressed Toola in Teja's clothes and jewellery and sent her with them. There was a resemblance between the two sisters—the unsuspecting prince even if he noticed a little change in her person attributed it to the few days' stay at her father's. The myna flew with them and took its shelter on the Royal terrace.

Teja, as you know, had left her weaving unfinished and now Toola had to continue it. She however was not an adept at weaving, but she tried her best to weave. The result however was that the thread and everything got all into a tangle. The myna, perched on a spot not very far, asked her to leave off weaving as she was only making a mess of the whole thing.

The prince happened to be near there, but though he was not a little surprised to hear the bird speak took no notice of it however.

On another occasion the prince happened to be playing dice with Toola after his midday repast. The myna flew to the spot where they were playing and sang out—

"Why art thou, O Prince, forgetful so,
That to play with wife's elder sister you go ?"

The prince did not take any notice of the bird's chirping at first—he was so busy with his game The myna however was persistent and it chirped again in the same strain This set him a-thinking for a while and going indoors he brought two sweets with him, one in each hand—one sweet was the hunger-sweet and the other was the thirst-sweet. Addressing the bird he said, "If thou be a stranger to me, O bird, thou wilt take this thirst-sweet from my hand and wilt fly away, but if thou be of my own kith and kin thou wilt take this hunger-sweet and wilt rest on my arm." On hearing which the bird flew to his hand at once and accepted the hunger-sweet,

He then began to stroke the bird affectionately

and while doing so he felt a pin on its head. He took it out and as he did so—lo and behold, there stood his own Teja before him. He was thunderstruck !

Teja then related to him all the incidents from the beginning to the end and as to her relationship with her step-mother.

The result was the prince commanded his executioner to behead Toola at once and to bring him her head, legs and hands in one jar, and her flesh in another and her blood in a third.

When this was done he commanded his messengers to carry these three receptacles to Toola's mother and present her with the two receptacles containing the flesh and blood, saying that they contained venison from the prince's park and the third one they were to retain and leave it at the door and take their departure before daybreak.

When Toola's mother saw that the prince's messengers were at the door with a hamper she was all agog with joy and said to herself, "That is just like my daughter" She said to herself, "She sends me a hamper immediately on her arrival, but the other one did not send me as much as a grain of corn."

All of them had a grand feast that night and

being in a generous mood she offered some of the venison to the messengers which however they declined, saying that they were too tired to eat anything that night.

Just before daybreak they left the jar containing Toola's head, legs and hands at the door as commanded by the prince. When she awoke in the morning Toola's mother's grief and consternation could be more easily imagined than described at the sight of the head, legs and hands in the jar.